First published: **September 2023**

55 Tufton Street
London SWIP 3QL

Email: books@civitas.org.uk

ISBN: 978-1-912581-49-8

Independence: Civitas: Institute for the Study of Civil Society is a registered educational charity (No. 1085494) and a company limited by guarantee (No. 04023541). Civitas is financed from a variety of private sources to avoid over-reliance on any single or small group of donors.

All the Institute's publications seek to further its objective of promoting the advancement of learning. The views expressed are those of the authors, not of the Institute.

Designed by Rubber Duckiee Ltd.

Printed in Great Britain
by 4edge Limited, Essex

'Islamophobia is rooted in racism and is a type of racism that targets expressions of Muslimness or perceived Muslimness'.

- APPG on British Muslims, Islamophobia Definition (from Islamophobia Defined)

Contents

Author

Hardeep Singh is a freelance journalist, Deputy-Director for the Network of Sikh Organisations and Assistant Editor of *The Sikh Messenger*. He was a leading member of the Libel Reform Campaign, along with science writer Simon Singh and cardiologist Dr Peter Wilmshurst. He co-authored the volume *Racialization, Islamophobia and Mistaken Identity: The Sikh Experience*. He co-authored the Civitas report *We Need to Check Your Thinking: How identity politics is warping police priorities from within* with Dr Richard Norrie. He is a contributing author to the volume *Legal Cases, New Religious Movements, and Minority Faiths.* He has written for *The Telegraph*, *The Spectator*, *Spiked*, *Quillette* and *The Critic* amongst others.

Foreword by Charles Moore

One should be wary when the word '-phobia' is stuck on to another word. It is a way of stigmatising the person accused of it and attacking his/her mental state rather than engaging with his/her opinions.

As has been well attested in much public argument, this is particularly true of the word 'Islamophobia'. Too often it has been deployed to silence discussion. Freedom of religion is rightly defended, but so must freedom of speech be. Freedom of speech is bound to involve the criticism of religion in general and sometimes of particular religions. All religions make certain truth claims. In a free society, people must be free to challenge these claims.

To argue that criticism of Muslim ideas is a form of racism is, in most cases, a profound mistake. If the APPG definition of Islamophobia were to prevail, our society would cease to put all religions on the same footing and would empower those unrepresentative Muslim leaders who are keenest to silence critics. Britain should not admit a blasphemy law by the back door (or by the front!).

Despite the Government's refusal to accept the APPG Islamophobia definition, some groups campaign relentlessly to change this. Hardeep Singh has a long, robust and deep engagement with these issues. He understands very well both the political and philosophical questions involved and the realities on the ground. His study of what is actually happening with questions of Islamophobia in too many local authorities in Britain makes worrying reading.

Hardeep Singh's thorough research in this report brings clarity and up-to-date information to the debate.

Charles Moore

Summary

- 15.6 per cent of local authorities in England who responded to Freedom of Information (FoI) requests have adopted the All-Party Parliamentary Group (APPG) on British Muslims definition of Islamophobia, despite central government rejecting it as 'not fit for purpose'.
- There is remarkably a panoply of alternative definitions of Islamophobia/anti-Muslim hatred adopted by several local authorities across England.
- Where opposition voices have been carefully considered, some councils have chosen not to formally adopt the APPG definition – this is highlighted by examples where the National Secular Society (NSS) has intervened.
- Concerns about the impact on free speech have been raised in meetings discussing the APPG definition in several local authorities.
- In Wales, the Senedd Commission's Diversity and Inclusion team has developed a glossary for the Commission that includes the APPG definition. The definition has been acknowledged by the Senedd's Race, Ethnicity and Cultural Heritage workplace network too. So, this could be viewed as adoption by the Welsh parliament via the back door.
- The widespread adoption of the APPG Islamophobia definition has been described by one councillor as part of a 'tide of little erosions', of which the overall effect is a 'dilution of one of our most precious values.'

Introduction

This report follows on from an earlier collection of essays on Islamophobia published by Civitas in August 2019. The anthology was compiled following concern about a working definition of Islamophobia as a 'type of racism' being adopted by local councils and political parties. At the time these included the Labour Party, Liberal Democrats, Plaid Cymru and the London Mayor's office, without necessary scrutiny or diligence, following publication of a 2018 report by the All-Party Parliamentary Group (APPG) on British Muslims – *Islamophobia Defined*. All of Scotland's political parties adopted the definition in 2019 too.[1] The Civitas anthology described the APPG definition as 'vague, expansive and unworkable', making many important observations, not least:

> *'The use of the term 'Muslimness' begs the question: who will be the arbiter of this? What about those Muslims who, to echo Baroness Falkner and Counter Extremism Commissioner Sara Khan,[2] are thought by other Muslims to be 'insufficiently Muslim'?* [3]

Who gets to qualify and decide 'Muslimness' and what it means remains a pertinent question today. As we will see, additional members of the Muslim community have subsequently objected to the term, as has a respected academic falsely accused of 'Islamophobia'. Its meaning has been questioned within local government too. The 2019 Civitas compilation captures concerns from academics, secularists, and individuals from a variety of faith backgrounds, most notably Muslims and an ex-Muslim. The present author was also a contributor to that anthology. These legitimate reservations, coupled with high-profile signatories to an accompanying letter to the then Home Secretary – Sajid Javid[4] – undoubtedly influenced policy makers.

In the end, the Conservative government chose not to adopt the APPG definition in 2019, as it conflated race and religion, as well as the serious implications it would have on free speech – be it academic freedom, legitimate discussion about aspects of Islamic doctrine, Islamic history, or investigative journalism focusing on Islamism. The dangerous implications of accusations of 'Islamophobia' to academic freedom are considered later, and best illustrated with reference to the troubling case of Professor Greer. In the end, the government said the APPG definition was 'not fit for purpose'.[5] Moreover, a report by Richard Walton and Tom Wilson for Policy Exchange – *Islamophobia – Crippling Counter-Terrorism* – starkly warned acceptance of the definition would, 'seriously undermine the effectiveness of the UK's counter-terrorism strategy (CONTEST) putting the country at greater risk from Islamist terrorism.'[6] However, following the government's rejection, the government initially indicated they would work with experts to come up with an alternative definition,[7] but these plans were dropped with an announcement last year,[8] and only one expert had ever been recruited in any case. As would be expected, the decision resulted in significant criticism from Muslim organisations,[9] and Muslim heritage opposition MPs in the Labour party.[10] [11] There are, as we will see, several alternative definitions for both 'Islamophobia' and 'anti-Muslim' hatred already being used and in circulation.

1 Kirkaldy, L. (2019) *All of Scotland's political parties adopt formal definition of Islamophobia*. Available at: holyrood.com/news/view,all-of-scotlands-political-parties-adopt-formal-definition-of-islamophobia_10221.htm (Accessed: 25 July 2023).

2 Now Dame Sara Khan.

3 *Hansard* HL Deb. vol. 794, 20 December 2018 [Online]. Available at: hansard.parliament.uk/lords/2018-12-20/debates/2F954D45-1962-4256-A492-22EB-F6AEF8F0/Islamophobia (Accessed: 25 July 2023).

4 Webb et al, *Open Letter: APPG Islamophobia Definition Threatens Civil Liberties*. Available at: civitas.org.uk (Accessed: 25 July 2023).

5 *Hansard* HC Deb. vol. 700, 9 September 2021. Available at: hansard.parliament.uk/commons/2021-09-09/debates/B2667B41-FDA9-4BFD-BCD3-AF-D4AF5165FD/DefinitionOfIslamophobia (Accessed: 25 July 2023).

6 Walton, R. and Wilson, T. (2019) *Islamophobia – Crippling Counter-Terrorism*, Policy Exchange. Available at: policyexchange.org.uk (Accessed: 25 July 2023).

7 Ministry of Housing, Communities & Local Government and Brokenshire, J. (2019) *New process set out to establish a working definition of Islamophobia*. Available at: gov.uk/government/news/new-process-set-out-to-establish-a-working-definition-of-islamophobia (Accessed: 25 July 2023).

8 Dearden, L. (2022) 'Government drops plan to combat anti-Muslim hatred with official definition of Islamophobia', *The Independent*, 30 October. Available at: independent.co.uk/news/uk/home-news/islamophobia-definition-conservative-government-michael-gove-b2213075.html (Accessed: 25 July 2023).

9 Ibid.

10 *Hansard* HC Debate vol.700, 9 September 2021 [Online] Available at: hansard.parliament.uk/commons/2021-09-09/debates/B2667B41-FDA9-4BFD-BCD3-AFD4AF5165FD/DefinitionOfIslamophobia (Accessed 18 August 2023).

11 Dearden, L. (2022) 'Government drops plan to combat anti-Muslim hatred with official definition of Islamophobia', *The Independent*, 30 October. Available at: independent.co.uk/news/uk/home-news/islamophobia-definition-conservative-government-michael-gove-b2213075.html (Accessed: 25 July 2023).

Indeed, there have been allegations of Islamophobia against both the Conservative and Labour parties. A review by Professor Swaran Singh – the *Independent Investigation into Alleged Discrimination*[12] (May 2021) – looked at high profile allegations, including 'Islamophobia' and other forms of discrimination within the Conservative and Unionist Party. One of its findings suggested:

> *'Anti-Muslim sentiment has been evidenced at local association and individual levels, as demonstrated by a number of social media complaints against Party members which were upheld by the Complaints Process'.*[13]

Anti-Muslim hatred and 'Islamophobia'

Whilst the vast majority in Britain are tolerant and believe in the principle of equality for all – there is an underbelly of society which holds contempt for minority groups, and the British Muslim communities are amongst those who have suffered from intolerance and prejudice. This has especially been the case following 9/11 and following a series of Islamic terrorist attacks domestically since, like 7/7, Lee Rigby, the Manchester arena bombing, the London Bridge attacks, Westminster Bridge attack, Fishmongers' Hall, and the murder of Sir David Amess[14] to name but a few. There are spikes in recorded anti-Muslim hate crime in the aftermath of terrorist attacks, and on their anniversaries.[15] There have been a series of high-profile incidents targeting members of the Muslim community in Britain, and overseas. The 2017 attack near Finsbury Park Mosque resulted in one death and 12 injured. The perpetrator Darren Osbourne was jailed for life for the attack. The sentencing judge Mrs Justice Cheema-Grubb said, 'this was a terrorist attack. You intended to kill'. [16] In New Zealand in 2019, 50 people were killed after a gunman opened fire at two Christchurch mosques. There were another 50 people injured, and one succumbed to their injuries later. The murder of innocent worshippers led to speedy reform of New Zealand's gun laws.[17]

The increasing role of hate crime law – and the new Race Equality Act

If we get a Labour government, they are likely to introduce a landmark Race Equality Act to tackle racism across society.[18] In opposition, Labour has endorsed the government rejected APPG definition of Islamophobia and has since introduced a code of conduct on Islamophobia,[19] which cites the APPG definition. If Islamophobia is considered to be 'a type of racism', then it is likely that a Labour government will look to include the contested APPG definition in official policy, perhaps even incorporate it into the Race Equality Act it has pledged to bring forth as a core commitment for its plans in government.

Although most hate crimes recorded in England and Wales are racially motivated, accounting for two thirds of statistics for 2021-22 (109,843 offences)[20] – religion is also one of the areas of priority for the government, with

12 The Singh Investigation (2021) *Independent Investigation into Alleged Discrimination*. Available at: singhinvestigation.co.uk (Accessed: 25 July 2023).

13 Ibid.

14 Dodd, V. (2022) 'Ali Harbi Ali guilty of murdering MP David Amess in terrorist attack', *The Guardian*, 11 April. Available at: theguardian.com/uk-news/2022/apr/11/david-amess-verdict-terrorist-attack-ali-harbi-ali-guilty (Accessed: 25 July 2023).

15 HCRW, *Anti-Muslim hate crime*. Available at: hatecrime.osce.org/anti-muslim-hate-crime (Accessed: 25 July 2023).

16 Rawlinson, K. (2018) 'Darren Osborne jailed for life for Finsbury Park terrorist attack', *The Guardian*, 2 February. Available at: theguardian.com/uk-news/2018/feb/02/finsbury-park-attack-darren-osborne-jailed (Accessed: 25 July 2023).

17 New Zealand Parliament (2021) *The Christchurch mosque attacks: how Parliament responded*. Available at: parliament.nz/mi/get-involved/features/the-christchurch-mosque-attacks-how-parliament-responded (Accessed: 25 July 2023).

18 Sudan, R. (2023) *Race Equality Act will be a "core part" of Labour's plans*. Available at: voice-online.co.uk/news/uk-news/2023/06/17/race-equality-act-will-be-a-core-part-of-labours-plans (Accessed: 25 July 2023).

19 Labour Party, *Code of Conduct: Islamophobia*. Available at: labour.org.uk/members/my-welfare/rules-and-codes-of-conduct/labours-islamophobia-policy (Accessed: 25 July 2023).

20 Home Office (2022) *Hate crime, England and Wales, 2021 to 2022*. Available at: gov.uk/government/statistics/hate-crime-england-and-wales-2021-to-2022/hate-crime-england-and-wales-2021-to-2022 (Accessed: 25 July 2023).

8,730 religious hate crimes recorded in the same period.[21] The joint ministerial forward to *Action Against Hate – The UK government's plan for tackling hate crime 'two years on'* (2018) proudly announced:

> *'...we were also the first country in the world to adopt the Working Definition of Antisemitism set out by the International Holocaust Remembrance Alliance, placing us firmly at the forefront of responding to community concerns.'*[22]

The government also set up funding to protect places of worship, or the Places of Worship: Protective Security Funding Scheme[23] – first announced in 2016 in *Action Against Hate* – the government's hate crime action plan. This involves the funding of CCTV cameras, security fencing, or other protective measures, where a legitimate need can be justified through an application process. Last year, the government announced that Mosques and Muslim faith schools would be given access to £24.5 million for security measures, and £3.5 million would be available for other faiths through the Places of Worship Fund.[24] The Muslim community, it was announced:

> *'...will be also able to register their interest in security guarding services at mosques, to ensure that their communities can worship safely and without fear.'*[25]

Security guard arrangements do not appear to be a taxpayer-funded option for other minority faiths. This £24.5 million funding commitment for Muslims was renewed in 2023. The government now name this as the 'Protective Security for Mosques Scheme'.[26] There is a separate (well-established) but parallel security funding stream for the Jewish community which runs alongside the Places of Worship Fund, with a sum of £14 million taxpayer funds provided last year,[27] and funding was increased by £1 million in 2023.[28]

Five monitored strands of hate crime exist for which the Home Office provides data – these are:[29]

- Race or ethnicity;
- Religion or beliefs;
- Sexual orientation;
- Disability; and
- Transgender identity.

The subject of this report focuses on religion. However, there is some indication from official statistics that, overall, we are becoming a less religious society. The 2021 census provides a fascinating insight into the religious constitution of England and Wales. Remarkably, less than half of the population (46.2 per cent, 27.5 million people) described themselves as 'Christian', which means Christianity is now a minority faith.[30] There has been a significant growth in those who categorise themselves with 'no religion' – the second most common

21 Ibid.

22 UK Government (2018) *Action Against Hate: The UK Government's plan for tackling hate crime – 'two years on'*. Available at: gov.uk (Accessed: 25 July 2023).

23 Home Office (2016) *Protective security schemes for places of worship*. Available at: gov.uk/guidance/places-of-worship-security-funding- scheme#:~:text=The%20Places%20of%20Worship%20Protective%20Security%20Funding%20Scheme%20provides%20funding,and%20associated%20faith%20community%20centre (Accessed: 25 July 2023).

24 Home Office and Hinds, D. (2022) *Places of Worship Protective Security Fund open for applications*. Available at: gov.uk/government/news/places-of-worship-protective-security-fund-open-for-applications--2 (Accessed: 25 July 2023).

25 Ibid.

26 Home Office and Tugendhat, T. (2023) *£28 million funding will help keep places of worship safe*. Available at: gov.uk/government/news/28-million-funding-will-help-keep-places-of-worship-safe (Accessed: 25 July 2023).

27 Home Office (2022) *Protective security grant funding for Jewish institutions to continue*. Available at: gov.uk/government/news/protective-security-grant-funding-for-jewish-institutions-to-continue (Accessed: 25 July 2023).

28 Home Office and Tugendhat, T. (2023) *£28 million funding will help keep places of worship safe*. Available at: gov.uk/government/news/28-million-funding-will-help-keep-places-of-worship-safe (Accessed: 25 July 2023).

29 Home Office (2022) *Hate crime, England and Wales, 2021 to 2022*. Available at: gov.uk/government/statistics/hate-crime-england-and-wales-2021-to-2022/hate-crime-england-and-wales-2021-to-2022 (Accessed: 25 July 2023).

30 ONS (2022) *Religion, England and Wales: Census 2021*. Available at: ons.gov.uk/peoplepopulationandcommunity/culturalidentity/religion/bulletins/religionenglandandwales/census2021 (Accessed: 25 July 2023).

choice. This increased by 12 percentage points to 37.2 per cent (22.2 million) from 25.2 per cent (14.1 million) in 2011.[31] The National Secular Society (NSS) called for a separate Church and state, based on the significant decline in Christianity.[32] Amongst the remaining faiths, Islam is the fastest growing religion in England and Wales, with 3.9 million people identifying as 'Muslim' – 6.5 per cent of the population in 2021, up from 2.7 million, 4.9 per cent, in 2011.[33] Other smaller minority faiths have seen a marginal increase, or no relative growth, versus the 2011 census figures. Jews, for example, have the same population percentage (0.5 per cent) as they did a decade prior, with 271,000[34] identifying as 'Jew' in 2021.[35] Hindus are 1.7 per cent of the population, with 1 million (an increase of 0.2 per cent), and Sikhs 0.9 per cent of the population with 524,000 – a marginal increase of 0.1 per cent from 2011.[36]

All police forces record data on race and religion, which is submitted to the Home Office – data which is included in national statistics. The National Police Chiefs' Council (NPCC) confirm that religious hate crime is disaggregated into crimes 'that are hostile to the larger religious groups (and no faith)', specifying that this includes Muslim and Jewish victims. Antisemitism data was published from 2008/9, in response to the then Government's adoption of the 2006 Antisemitism APPG report.[37] Amongst the faith groups, Jews and Muslims are the only two in Britain who have specific definitions of hate crime officially recognised – and adopted by public bodies – either central government, local government, or universities. The International Holocaust Remembrance Alliance (IHRA) definition of antisemitism was adopted by the government in December 2016.[38] On adoption of the IHRA the Prime Minister at the time, Theresa May, said:

> *'...there will be one definition of anti-Semitism – in essence, language or behaviour that displays hatred towards Jews because they are Jews – and anyone guilty of that will be called out on it.'*[39]

In December 2019, the then Communities Secretary, Robert Jenrick, wrote to Leaders of Councils urging the adoption of the IHRA definition of antisemitism and the working examples. Government agreement around a definition of 'Islamophobia' has, however, been contested and controversial. As well as researching local authority (LA) uptake of the APPG definition, this research analyses LA's who have accepted or rejected the IHRA definition too. This comparator was included to consider potential trends, for example were both definitions adopted simultaneously, did the uptake of the IHRA influence the subsequent adoption of the APPG, and in the case of the IHRA, did central government adoption influence LA uptake?

There have been limited efforts to recognise hate crime against other minority faiths. In a 2020 Islamophobia debate, crossbencher Lord Singh of Wimbledon reminded the government of their commitment, 'to protect all religions and beliefs without fear or favour'[40] – essentially a plea for a level playing field. In a 2018 debate, he made the point that, 'groups without a culture of complaint, such as Sikhs, fall off the Government's radar.'[41] The volume *Racialization, Islamophobia and Mistaken Identity The Sikh Experience* by Jhutti-Johal and Singh highlights this ongoing blind spot in public policy. The APPG for British Sikhs' effort in defining 'anti-Sikh hate',[42]

31 Ibid.

32 National Secular Society (2022) *Census England & Wales: Less than half the population Christian*. Available at: secularism.org.uk/news/2022/11/census-england-and-wales-less-than-half-the-population-christian (Accessed: 25 July 2023).

33 Ibid.

34 Ibid.

35 Ibid.

36 Ibid.

37 All-Party Parliamentary Group Against Antisemitism (2006) *Report of the All-Party Parliamentary Inquiry into Antisemitism*. Available at: archive.jpr.org.uk/download?id=1274 (Accessed: 25 July 2023).

38 Torrance, D. (2018) *UK Government's adoption of the IHRA definition of antisemitism*. Available at: commonslibrary.parliament.uk/uk-governments-adoption-of-the-ihra-definition-of-antisemitism (Accessed: 25 July 2023).

39 Prime Minister's Office et al. (2016) *Government leads the way in tackling anti-Semitism*. Available at: gov.uk/government/news/government-leads-the-way-in-tackling-anti-semitism (Accessed: 25 July 2023).

40 *Hansard* HL Deb. vol.801, 13 February 2020 [Online] Available at: hansard.parliament.uk/lords/2020-02-13/debates/D2C6CF82-DDBD-4AB5-949D-C1205E3AF0A4/Islamophobia (Accessed: 18 August 2023).

41 *Hansard* HL Deb. vol. 794, 20 December 2018 [Online]. Available at: hansard.parliament.uk/lords/2018-12-20/debates/2F954D45-1962-4256-A492-22EB-F6AEF8F0/Islamophobia (Accessed: 25 July 2023).

42 All-Party Parliamentary Group for British Sikhs (2020) *A report into anti-Sikh hate crimes*. Available at: http://www.sikhfeduk.com (Accessed: 25 July 2023).

[43] however, fell short. Mainly because the definition failed to capture cases of 'mistaken identity' – where Sikhs, by virtue of their turbans and beards, are confused with extremist Muslims, like Al Qaeda operatives, the Taliban, or Islamic State (IS). Furthermore, it conflated racial and religious hatred, which is unsurprising, given the APPG secretariat[44] previously led a failed campaign to secure a Sikh 'ethnic' tick box in the 2021 Census. This, despite 'Sikh' already existing as an option under religion.

Following the civil unrest in Leicester last year between Hindu and Muslim communities, there have been some efforts to highlight anti-Hindu hate. A report by the Henry Jackson Society (HJS) investigated discrimination against Hindu pupils in schools in the UK,[45] with some Hindu groups pushing to secure a UK government recognised definition of 'Hinduphobia.'[46] At the time of writing, this doesn't appear to have progressed in a meaningful way. *The Bloom Review – Does government 'do God?'*[47] rightly emphasised the importance of improving 'faith literacy' across the parliamentary estate. It is the view of the author that working towards parity in addressing hate crime for all faiths and none, or simply understanding how different communities are impacted in the first instance, should be factored into this education.

Indeed, prejudice and discrimination targeting faith is a serious issue, as demonstrated by government statistics referenced above. However, unlike other 'crimes' where a decrease in statistics demonstrates success in tackling crime, the state wants to demonstrate an increase in recording and reporting of hate crimes. This occurs, in part, through third-party reporting organisations which receive government funding – for example, Community Security Trust (CST)[48] and Tell MAMA (Measuring Anti-Muslim Attacks).[49] Last year, Minister Kemi Badenoch confirmed, 'we [the government] have supported Tell MAMA with just over £4 million between 2016 and 2022 to monitor and combat anti-Muslim hatred'.[50] Here, it is important to reflect on Joanna Williams' observation in *Policing Hate*:

> *'...that whereas police statistics show year-on-year increases in recorded hate crimes, CSEW (Crime Survey for England and Wales) data suggests the opposite, that the longer term trend is for a reduction in the number of hate crime incidents'.*[51]

Alongside serious incidents recorded by the police, trivial incidents like a verbal dispute at a supermarket checkout, with use of religious epithets, could also qualify as a hate crime statistic. In *How hate crime policy is undermining our law and society*, Richard Norrie makes this very point having analysed details of a variety of incidents disclosed by the police. He says:

> *'...note that something as little as telling someone to 'XXXX Off' in an argument over a car parking space is sufficient for a race hate crime to be recorded. There is no evidence of racial slurs or even a crime in that example.'*

43 'Anti-Sikh hate' is any incident or crime which is perceived by the victim or any other person to be religiously or racially motivated by hostility, hatred or prejudice against Sikhs or those perceived to be Sikh people, Gurdwaras, organisations or property.

44 Parallel Parliament (2023) *British Sikhs APPG*. Available at: parallelparliament.co.uk/APPG/british-sikhs (Accessed: 25 July 2023).

45 Littlewood, C. (2023) *Anti-Hindu Hate in Schools*. Available at: henryjacksonsociety.org/publications/anti-hindu-hate-in-schools (Accessed: 25 July 2023).

46 Global Hindu Federation, *Anti Hinduism/Hinduphobia Definition launched at BBC Protest*. Available at: globalhindufederation.org/ghf-uk-campaigns/anti-hinduism-hinduphobia-definition-launched-at-bbc-protest (Accessed: 25 July 2023).

47 Department for Levelling Up, Housing and Communities and Baroness Scott of Bybrook OBE (2023) *Government needs to better understand faith, independent review claims*. Available at: gov.uk/government/news/government-needs-to-better-understand-faith-independent-review-claims (Accessed: 25 July 2023).

48 CST, *Reporting Antisemitic incidents to CST*. Available at: cst.org.uk/report-incident (Accessed: 25 July 2023).

49 Tell MAMA. Available at: tellmamauk.org (Accessed: 25 July 2023).

50 *Hansard* HC Deb. vol. 710, 7 March 2022 [Online]. Available at: hansard.parliament.uk/commons/2022-03-07/debates/61686F01-0F8B-4D98-BBC0-761078F481BF/Islamophobia (Accessed: 25 July 2023).

51 Williams, J. (2020) *Policing Hate*, Civitas. Available at: civitas.org.uk (Accessed: 25 July 2023).

What counts as a hate crime is then something open for debate. In 2021, Donna Jones, lead on serious and organised crime for the Association of Police and Crime Commissioners, said doubling of hate crime reflected police activity rather than real events.[52] Suffice to say, we must read into these statistics with some caution.

The latest Home Office statistics (year ending March 2022) show that 42 per cent of victims experiencing recorded religious hate crime are perceived to be Muslims. This is the highest number for any faith group. Hate crimes against Jews in 2021/22 comes next, making up nearly a quarter of all religious hate crimes reported nationally. However, as previously discussed, non-Muslims (including those of no faith) are also perceived to be Muslims and thus get recorded under the 'Islamophobic' hate crime flag. Data on the 'perceived' versus 'actual' victim is not however currently published by the Home Office annually – and it is something that the government should obtain from police forces and publish for the sake of openness and transparency.

A request under the Freedom of Information Act was put to the Home Office asking:

> *'For the year ending March 2022, out of the 3,459 religious hate crime offences where the perceived religion of the victim was Muslim, how many:*
>
> *'(i) are non-Muslims victims, or those of no recorded faith;*
>
> *'(ii) Muslim victims with Muslim perpetrators.'*

It was responded to as follows:

> *'The Home Office collects the targeted or perceived religion of the victim but the actual religion is not routinely supplied to the Home Office by police forces in England and Wales. Information on offenders is the responsibility of the Ministry of Justice.'*

Indeed, the same 'perception' based principle would apply to a heterosexual leaving a gay nightclub and being assaulted, based on the perception he or she is homosexual. The victim is heterosexual, but the crime will inevitably be recorded as 'homophobic'.

As indicated, it is also worth noting that some 'Islamophobic' crimes are likely to capture sectarianism within the Muslim community itself. This was confirmed to be the case at a Crown Prosecution Service (CPS) National Scrutiny Panel focused on religiously aggravated hate crime, attended by the present author last year. In its worst manifestation, this has led to the murder of the Ahmadiyya Glaswegian shopkeeper Asad Shah in 2016,[53] and the murder of a Sufi Imam in the same year, for 'purely sectarian reasons' according to the BBC.[54] Protests outside cinemas against the 'blasphemous' film *The Lady of Heaven,* which looked at early Islamic history through a Shia prism, resulted in UK cinemas withdrawing it. One Muslim critic said the film was 'underpinned with a sectarian ideology.'[55]

Both antisemitism and Islamophobia are terms with broad recognition and reference – and the subject of significant academic research, analysis, government debate and media coverage. An audit previously conducted by the present author demonstrated in 2014-15 there were 262 articles in UK national newspapers which mentioned the word 'Islamophobia' and 328 in 2016-17 – of those, 17.5 per cent and 11.2 per cent, respectively, also referred to antisemitism.[56] Suffice to say, there are significant column inches dedicated to hate crime targeting both Muslims and Jewish communities.

52 Hymas, C. (2021) 'Hate crimes risk distracting police from focusing on serious offences, warns policing chief', *The Telegraph*, 24 October. Available at: telegraph.co.uk/news/2021/10/24/hate-crimes-risk-distracting-police-focusing-serious-offences (Accessed: 25 July 2023).

53 BBC News (2016) *Asad Shah killing: 'Disrespecting Islam' murderer jailed*. Available at: bbc.co.uk/news/uk-scotland-glasgow-west-37021385 (Accessed: 25 July 2023).

54 BBC News (2016) *Jalal Uddin murder: Syeedy guilty over Rochdale imam death*. Available at: bbc.com/news/uk-england-manchester-37388073 (Accessed: 25 July 2023).

55 Whitbread, D. and Sharman, J. (2022) ''Blasphemy' protesters force Cineworld to drop film about prophet Muhammad's daughter', *The Independent*, 8 June. Available at: independent.co.uk/news/uk/home-news/lady-of-heaven-film-blasphemy-protest-b2095822.html (Accessed: 25 July 2023).

56 Jhutti-Johal, J. and Singh, H. (2020) *Racialization, Islamophobia and Mistaken Identity: The Sikh Experience*. Routledge.

In contrast, faith groups like Christians, Hindus and Sikhs do not have terms officially recognised definitions for prejudice targeting them with working examples adopted by statutory bodies. The decimation of Christianity in the Middle East, and massacre of Christians in Nigeria – described as 'genocide in slow motion' – [57] is rarely referred as 'Christianophobia', nor is the arrest or prosecution of Christian street preachers here for alleged breaches of the Public Order Act here for causing 'alarm' or 'distress'. Media coverage of the stabbing in 2021 of Hatun Tash, a Christian speaker at Speakers' Corner,[58] as well as reports in 2023 of a plan to kill her in a terrorist attack, followed a similar pattern.[59] [60]

What could be the reason for this? In *Is Identity Politics Undermining Police Impartiality?* David Green summarises 10 Critical Race Theory (CRT) assertions in Özlem Sensoy and Robin DiAngelo's book *Is Everyone Really Equal? An Introduction to Key Concepts in Social Justice Education*. The tenth reads:

> '*...because dominant groups occupy the positions of power, their members receive social advantages, Cis-Men, whites, heterosexuals, the able-bodied, Christians and upper classes automatically receive privilege by being members of a dominant group.*'

This theory seems to support the frankly absurd view that not all victims are equal – and those deemed the 'oppressor', by virtue of being 'dominant', cannot even be considered 'victim'. The universal truth is that all human beings suffer the pangs of hurting and misfortune, including manifestations of prejudice and hatred – it is part and parcel of our human experience. Asserting this view alone would likely be viewed as the ultimate blasphemy for those who adhere to the cult of progressivism.

Moreover, as my previous research on London has demonstrated – 28 per cent of recorded perception-based 'Islamophobic' hate crime victims recorded by the Metropolitan Police in 2015, and 25 per cent in 2016, were in fact against non-Muslims, or no known or recorded religion.[61] This included Christians, Hindus, Sikhs, Jews, Buddhists, and Atheists – but these victims continue to remain hidden in media reports. The *Evening Standard* acknowledged these statistics following a complaint from the author making an amendment to an article titled 'Anti-Muslim hate crimes increase fivefold since London Bridge attacks', whereas *The Guardian* chose to ignore a similar complaint. So, if a Sikh, Rastafarian, or Coptic Christian priest is abused and referred to as 'Bin Laden' or 'Taliban', that is likely to be recorded under an 'Islamophobic' hate crime flag – the perception being the victim was targeted due to being mistaken for a Muslim extremist. Notably, the Sikh issue gets a passing mention in one London council, as we will observe later.

De facto blasphemy laws?

The Rushdie affair was sparked by the publication of the novel *The Satanic Verses* back in 1988. However, in recent years we have seen cases which beg the question whether a de facto blasphemy law exists in relation to Islam. In October 2020, teacher Samuel Paty was stabbed and beheaded near his school in the town of Conflans-Sainte-Honorine, near Paris. He was murdered by a Muslim extremist for having shown cartoons of

57 Singh, H. (2023) 'When will the world wake up to the persecution of Nigerian Christians?', *The Spectator*, 4 July. Available at: spectator.co.uk/article/when-will-the-world-wake-up-to-the-persecution-of-nigerian-christians (Accessed: 25 July 2023).

58 O'Reilly, E. (2021) 'An interview with Hatun Tash, the Christian preacher stabbed at Speakers' Corner', *The Spectator*, 10 August. Available at: spectator.co.uk/article/an-interview-with-hatun-tash-the-christian-preacher-stabbed-at-speakers-corner (Accessed: 25 July 2023).

59 BBC News (2023) *Speakers' Corner: Man admits Hyde Park gun attack plot*. Available at: bbc.com/news/uk-england-london-65646464 (Accessed: 25 July 2023).

60 Nor is the ethnic cleansing of Sikhs in Afghanistan referred to as 'Sikhophobia'. Although the exact numbers are difficult to confirm, a recent UK Home Office report estimates that, before 1992, there may have been as many as 220,000 Hindus and Sikhs in Afghanistan. A 2022 BBC report indicates 140 Sikhs were left in Kabul.

61 Kakar, A. (2018) 'Guardian accused of self-regulation failure by Network of Sikh Organisations over hate crime complaint', *Press Gazette*, 22 March. Available at: pressgazette.co.uk/publishers/nationals/guardian-accused-of-self-regulation-failure-by-network-of-sikh-organisations-over-hate-crime-complaint (Accessed: 25 July 2023).

the Prophet Mohammad during a class on freedom of expression.[62] The murder of Paty follows the 2015 Charlie Hebdo terror attack resulting in a massacre at the offices of satirical magazine.[63] The controversial publication had previously published cartoons mocking the Prophet.

The accusation of blasphemy has led to threats of violence in relation to depictions of the Prophet Muhammad in cartoons, or incidents of sacrilege against the Quran, and is something that has played out in British schools. In Batley Grammar, West Yorkshire, a teacher was forced into hiding after showing the caricature during a religious studies lesson in March 2021. Protestors gathered outside the school, the teacher was suspended, and it was reported he was moved into police protection. The head teacher issued an unequivocal apology[64] and the teacher remains in hiding today. In 2023, an autistic schoolboy in Kettlethorpe High School (also in West Yorkshire) received 'death threats' for accidentally scuffing a Quran, despite there being 'no malicious intent.'[65] The police recorded the scuffing as a 'hate incident', which received criticism from the Free Speech Union.[66] In *We Need to Check Your Thinking!,*[67] Norrie and Singh previously recommended that the College of Policing's invention of Non-Crime Hate Incidents (NCHIs) be scrapped, and this example highlights another good reason why. The boy's safety and wellbeing should have taken precedent over hurt feelings. A recent Henry Jackson Society report has warned that anti-blasphemy protests outside schools (like Batley Grammar) and cinemas by hardliners, 'pose [a] national security threat'.[68]

Indeed, the attempted murder of Sir Salman Rushdie in New York last year starkly highlights how accusations of blasphemy and 'offence' translate into real-world violence.[69] But do we now have a de facto blasphemy law in place? Blasphemy has been taken off the statute books, most recently with the passing of the Hate Crime and Public Order (Scotland) Act 2021. However, the mere accusation of 'Islamophobia' alone can have serious and dangerous implications for those on the sharp end. Former Head of the Equality and Human Rights Commission (EHRC), Trevor Phillips, said his nomination for the annual controversial and satirical 'Islamophobe of the year' award in 2017 'put target on [my] back'.[70] It is extraordinary to ponder that Phillips was the individual who is largely responsible for the introduction of the word 'Islamophobia'[71] into the lexicon, following the publication of the Runnymede report – *Islamophobia: a challenge for us all* (1997).[72] Accusations of 'Islamophobia' later got him suspended from the Labour Party in 2020. A high-profile opponent of the APPG definition, he described his suspension as 'pure political gangsterism'.[73] The suspension was subsequently lifted.[74]

62 France24 (2021) *'The violence shook me profoundly': Teachers, students remember Samuel Paty's murder.* Available at: france24.com/en/france/20211015-the-violence-shook-me-profoundly-teachers-students-remember-samuel-paty-s-murder (Accessed: 25 July 2023).

63 Salaun, T. (2020) *Charlie Hebdo attackers killed to avenge Prophet Mohammad, French court hears.* Available at: reuters.com/article/uk-france-charlieheb-do-trial-idUKKBN25S6B1 (Accessed: 25 July 2023).

64 Teale, C. (2021) 'Batley head teacher issues 'unequivocal apology' for use of 'completely inappropriate' Prophet Muhammad cartoon in RS', *Yorkshire Live*, 25 March. Available at: examinerlive.co.uk/news/west-yorkshire-news/batley-head-teacher-issues-unequivocal-20256891 (Accessed: 25 July 2023).

65 Haigh, E. and Brooke, C. (2023) 'Boy who 'accidentally dropped a copy of the Quran at Wakefield school' receives 'death threats': Teenager is left 'absolutely petrified' by messages, says mother', *Daily Mail*, 1 March. Available at: dailymail.co.uk/news/article-11809601/Boy-dropped-copy-Quran-Wakefield-school-left-petrified-death-threats.html (Accessed: 25 July 2023).

66 Ibid.

67 Norrie, R. and Singh, H. (2022) *We Need to Check Your Thinking: How identity politics is warping police priorities from within*, Civitas. Available at: civitas.org.uk (Accessed: 25 July 2023).

68 Johnston, N. (2023) 'Protests outside schools and cinemas by hardline Muslims 'pose national security threat'', *The Telegraph*, 17 July. Available at: telegraph.co.uk/news/2023/07/17/islamic-protests-uk-schools-blasphemy-security-threat-warn (Accessed: 25 July 2023).

69 Saunders, E. (2023) *Sir Salman Rushdie speaks for the first time about 'colossal attack'.* Available at: bbc.com/news/entertainment-arts-64537770 (Accessed: 25 July 2023).

70 Hellen, N. (2017) 'Islamophobia award 'puts target on back' of former equalities chief Trevor Phillips', *The Times*, 26 November. Available at: thetimes.co.uk/article/islamophobia-award-puts-target-on-back-of-former-equalities-chief-5j3swc7dg (Accessed: 25 July 2023).

71 The Runnymede report (1997) provided the following definition of Islamophobia, along with a summary of criticisms of the term: 'Islamophobia refers to unfounded hostility towards Islam. It refers also to the practical consequences of such hostility in unfair discrimination against Muslim individuals and communities, and to the exclusion of Muslims from mainstream political and social affairs. The term is not, admittedly, ideal. Critics of it consider that its use panders to what they call political correctness, that is stifles legitimate criticism of Islam, and that it demonises and stigmatises anyone who wishes to engage in such criticism.'

72 The Runnymede Trust (1997) *Islamophobia: A Challenge For Us All.* Available at: runnymedetrust.org (Accessed: 26 July 2023).

73 Grice, A. (2020) 'The Trevor Phillips Islamophobia row proves Labour has a long road back to power', *The Independent*, 9 March. Available at: independent.co.uk/voices/trevor-phillips-islamophobia-labour-leadership-corbyn-racism-rotherham-ehrc-a9387746.html (Accessed: 26 July 2023).

74 Siddique, H. (2021) 'Labour lifts Trevor Phillips' suspension for alleged Islamophobia', *The Guardian*, 6 July. Available at: theguardian.com/uk-news/2021/jul/06/labour-lifts-trevor-phillips-suspension-for-alleged-islamophobia (Accessed: 26 July 2023).

There is also a serious threat to academic freedom, which is best illustrated by the troubling case of Professor Greer. Author of *Falsely Accused of Islamophobia: My Struggle Against Academic Cancellation,*[75] Greer said a complaint from the University of Bristol Islamic Society (BRISOC) made against him was a 'potentially life-threatening campaign... based on nothing but lies, distortion and misrepresentation.'[76] Following a suspicious incident after a media report on his case, Greer and his wife decided to temporarily leave home for fear of their safety. Changing his appearance with a long 'Taliban like' beard, and thick spectacles, he felt compelled to carry a screwdriver for his own protection. In October 2021, he was cleared of the accusation, but a module which he taught was pulled regardless, despite no evidence of 'Islamophobia'. Greer, an expert in criminal justice, human rights, law, and counterterrorism, alleges Bristol university 'mishandled' his case, whilst failing to punish the students behind the malicious complaint. He described his experience as 'terrifying'.[77]

In relation to the APPG definition, Greer told me:

> *'"Muslimness" Is a fake concept insofar as it's an attempt to ascribe an ethnic identity to a faith. "Muslimness" is an affiliation to faith, not an ethnic identity.'*

As previously discussed, the APPG definition creates a standard by which blasphemy risks being enforced, through its vagueness. During a debate on Islamophobia in the House of Lords in 2018, the incumbent EHRC chief, Baroness Falkner, made a similar point to Greer when she said:

> *'When you define a religion – in other words, a belief system – as an adjective [Muslimness] and declare that this is rooted in race, which is biological, you ascribe to belief an immutability which cannot work.'*[78]

Greer said Bristol West is one of the safest Labour seats in the country, but he has not yet sought to involve the local MP Thangam Debbonaire (Bristol University falls within her constituency) but indicated he might still do so. A fascinating aspect in the Greer case is that the complainants, the BRISOC, did not endorse the APPG definition following the university's adoption post complaint. Instead, like the Conservative government (although for different reasons) they described it as 'not fit for purpose'. As outlined in Greer's book, BRISOC took the following view:

> *'The recent adoption of the All Party Parliamentary Group (APPG) definition of Islamophobia has had no effect in practice and we feel that it is now our representative responsibility to highlight how the APPG definition of Islamophobia seeks to protect no one and is wholly not fit for purpose in addressing our experiences of Islamophobia, coupled with the fact that according to the university implementation of policies to protect students have to be 'balanced' with "academic freedom".'*[79]

There is no doubt that academic freedom must be protected and is under threat – the appalling treatment of both Greer, and former Sussex University gender-critical academic Kathleen Stock, are of course not isolated cases.[80] Although BRISOC does not appear to support the APPG definition, they did of course use the term 'Islamophobia', which conflates anti-Muslim hatred with criticism of Islam, and/or the behaviour of extremists. As previously noted, 'Islamophobia' could also describe sectarianism within the Muslim community, and covers non-Muslims being targeted on the basis they are perceived to be Muslim in so-called 'mistaken identity' incidents. One could then fairly describe 'Islamophobia' as a 'catch-all' term.

75 Greer, S. (2023) *Falsely Accused of Islamophobia: My Struggle Against Academic Cancellation (Revised and Expanded Paperback Edition)* Academia Press.

76 BBC News (2023) *University of Bristol professor's anger at Islamophobia claim*. Available at: bbc.com/news/uk-england-bristol-64704670 (Accessed: 26 July 2023).

77 Ibid.

78 *Hansard* HL Deb. vol. 794, 20 December 2018 [Online]. Available at: hansard.parliament.uk/lords/2018-12-20/debates/2F954D45-1962-4256-A492-22EB-F6AEF8F0/Islamophobia (Accessed: 25 July 2023).

79 Greer, S. (2023) *Falsely Accused of Islamophobia: My Struggle Against Academic Cancellation (Revised and Expanded Paperback Edition)* Academia Press.

80 In May 2023, Rishi Sunak announced the appointment of the first free speech tsar, who will have the power to investigate universities who censor academics.

In a talk on Islamic extremism back in 2009, the late Christopher Hitchens warned an audience, 'resist it while you still can and before the right to complain is taken away from you, which will be the next thing'.[81] He prophetically added:

> *'[Y]ou will be told you can't complain because you're Islamophobic – the term is already being introduced into the culture as if it were an accusation of race hatred for example, or bigotry.'*

Putin's reference to 'Western elites' as 'Russophobic'[82] provides another contemporary example of the deployment of charged terms which ultimately serve to distract opponents from legitimately criticising bad behaviour, not least, in Putin's case, the invasion of Ukraine.

Adoption of the APPG definition by political parties

We have already examined adoption by all the main political parties in Westminster and Scotland despite the Conservative government's rejection of the APPG Islamophobia definition. This also did not prevent the Green Party from doing the same in December 2022.[83] Notably the Green Party decision included an addendum, in which they flag the Federation of Student Islamic Societies' (FOSIS) concerns about the APPG definition – which relate specifically to its conflation of race and religion. The document reads, 'this addendum is intended to acknowledge the range of concerns about the definition', and goes onto say the party 'will keep the definition of Islamophobia under review.'[84] What this 'review' encompasses or how often it will be conducted remains unclear, however the statement indicates a hint of doubt, and brings into question why the definition was endorsed by the Green Party in the first place.

In 2019 Anas Sarwar MSP – now leader of the Scottish Labour Party – led a cross party group in Holyrood, urging adoption of the APPG definition by the Scottish government and Scottish councils.[85] The Holyrood group worked with the APPG on British Muslims. Sarwar was joined by Conservative peer – Baroness Warsi – in Scotland, calling for a definition to be officially adopted.[86] The definition was endorsed by all Scottish political parties. The then First Minister, Nicola Sturgeon, indicated she wanted the Scottish government to formally adopt it, which triggered protest from the Scottish Humanist Society.[87] Sarwar pressed the government with questions in February 2022, asking:

> *'[W]hether it [The Scottish government] will commit to adopting the All-Party Parliamentary Group on British Muslims' definition of Islamophobia, and, if so, within what timeframe.'*[88]

On 3 March 2022, Alex Cole-Hamilton MSP, Leader of the Scottish Liberal Democrats, submitted a motion in the Scottish Parliament requesting all local councils to adopt the definition, in addition to accompanying guidelines put together by a group called the Coalition Against Islamophobia. It was supported by 14 MSPs, including

81 TimothyWarke (2018) *Christopher Hitchens on Islamophobia (2009)*. Available at: youtube.com/watch?v=0EYg8Tgrh0o (Accessed: 26 July 2023).

82 Browning, O. (2023) 'Putin accuses 'Western elites' of encouraging 'Russophobia' during Victory Day speech', *The Independent*, May. Available at: independent.co.uk/tv/news/russia-vladimir-putin-victory-day-speech-b2335372.html (Accessed: 26 July 2023).

83 Alston, S. (2023) *Green Party adopts APPG definition of Islamophobia*. Available at: bright-green.org/2023/03/23/green-party-adopts-appg-definition-of-islamophobia (Accessed: 18 August 2023).

84 Green Party (2022) *GPRC Approved Addendum to the All-Party Parliamentary Group on British Muslims' Definition of Islamophobia*. Available at: members.greenparty.org.uk (Accessed: 18 August 2023).

85 Paterson, S. (2019) 'MSP in call for islamophobia definition to be adopted in Scotland to tackle racism and hate', *The Glasgow Times*, 26 April. Available at: glasgowtimes.co.uk/news/17598498.msp-call-islamophobia-definition-adopted-scotland-tackle-racism-hate (Accessed: 18 August 2023).

86 Ibid.

87 Humanist Society Scotland (2019) *We voice concern about adopted definition of Islamophobia*. Available at: humanism.scot/2019/04/26/humanists-voice-concern-on-adopted-definition-of-islamophobia (Accessed: 26 July 2023).

88 Scottish Parliament (2022) *S6W-06439*. Questions asked by Anas Sarwar, 10 February. Question answered by Shona Robinson, 10 March. Available at: parliament.scot/chamber-and-committees/questions-and-answers/question?ref=s6w-06439 (Accessed: 26 July 2023).

Sarwar.[89] The Scottish government responded to the question on whether they had adopted the APPG definition, with:

> *'[W]e previously consulted with communities affected by Islamophobia on whether a definition would be helpful in Scotland, and although communities were broadly supportive of a definition, there was no consensus on the All-Party Parliamentary Group (APPG) definition.'*

In Wales, Plaid Cymru adopted the APPG definition of Islamophobia. In a tabled question, Leanne Wood AM asked the Deputy Minister:

> *'Will the Welsh Government make a statement on the impact that the UK Government's rejection of the definition of Islamophobia has had on community cohesion'?*[90]

The Minister confirmed that the Welsh government was in discussion with the Scottish government, 'with a view to adopting the definition'.[91] In a response to a Freedom of Information (FoI) request as to whether the Welsh parliament had adopted the APPG definition, the following response was given. This could be viewed as adoption by the back door:

> *'Thank you for contacting the Welsh Parliament regarding your enquiry into the Senedd's definition of Islamophobia. The Senedd Commission has not officially adopted a definition of Islamophobia. The Commission's Diversity and Inclusion team has developed a glossary for Commission that includes the following definition, which is the same as that noted below: Islamophobia is rooted in racism and is a type of racism that targets expressions of Muslimness or perceived Muslimness. The glossary has not yet been published, but the definition has been acknowledged by the Senedd's Race Ethnicity and Cultural Heritage workplace network.'*

On matters such as this, devolved governments can of course make their independent decisions, but what is remarkable is the uptake of the APPG definition by local government in England, Wales, and Scotland, despite central government rejection. How this has played out could be in part attributed to party politics – but it is also because of the phenomenon referred to as 'virtue signalling'. To be seen to be doing the 'right thing' is all that is required to be virtuous, regardless of real-world implications, not least the serious implications to free speech.

Through a series of FoI requests to local authorities across England, Wales, and Scotland, this research provides an insight into the level of uptake of the APPG Islamophobia definition across local government in each country. Adoption of the definition is limited, but nevertheless significant, and it is fair to say it has taken on a life of its own.

89 Scottish Parliament (2022) Motion submitted by Cole-Hamilton, A. et al. *S6M-03357*. Available at: parliament.scot/chamber-and-committees/votes-and-motions/S6M-03357 (Accessed: 26 July 2023).

90 Welsh Parliament (2019) *Plenary - Fifth Senedd*, 22 May. Available at: record.senedd.wales/Plenary/5658#C196565 (Accessed: 26 July 2023).

91 Ibid.

The approaches of local government towards Islamophobia

According to the Institute for Government, there are 333 local authorities in England. The structure of local government varies between them. You have two-tiers areas (county and district councils) and single tier (32 London boroughs, 36 metropolitan districts, 58 unitary authorities). There are 32 councils in Scotland, which are all unitary authorities. There are 22 local authorities (unitary) in Wales.[92] A total of 369 FoI requests were submitted to councils across England (318), Wales (21) and Scotland (30) via direct email or the council's online portal. Twenty-nine councils did not reply to FoIs in England. We were not able to file FoIs for 13 councils in England, one in Wales, and two in Scotland. Some councils responded confirming they do not hold the information requested, or the terms 'antisemitism' or 'Islamophobia' do not come up in searches of council minutes. This was taken to be non-adoption.

The FoIs were filed prior to the 31 March 2023; and because of local government reorganisation, some councils that previously existed at the time of the FoI requests ceased to exist after the 31 March 2023. For example, with the formation of the North Yorkshire Council (a new unitary authority), Hambleton District Council ceased to exist post 31 March 2023. Cumbria and Somerset County councils were also restructured into unitary authorities in April 2023.[93] The councils were also classified according to the political party with overall control prior to the local elections in May 2023, so this does not necessarily reflect the current political control everywhere. In those elections Labour won several councils from no overall control (NOC), including Plymouth, Stoke-on-Trent, Blackpool, Middlesbrough, Broxtowe, High Peak and North East Derbyshire.[94] The Labour Party lost overall control in other councils, like its former stronghold Slough.[95]

The following questions were submitted to councils in England, Wales and Scotland under the FoI Act 2000, and FoI (Scotland) Act 2002, respectively.

(1) Has the council adopted the APPG on British Muslims definition of Islamophobia from the report Islamophobia Defined? The definition in question is: 'Islamophobia is rooted in racism and is a type of racism that targets expressions of Muslimness or perceived Muslimness'.

(2) If yes, when was it adopted and was it following a unanimous vote? An indication of the votes for and against would be helpful.

(3) Please can you share any minutes of meetings from the discussion of the definition prior to the vote, in the event it was adopted, or rejected subsequently.

(4) Has the council also adopted the IHRA working definition of antisemitism?

92 Paun, A., Wilson, J. and Hall, D. (2019) *Local government.* Available at: institutefor government.org.uk/explainer/local-government (Accessed: 26 July 2023).

93 Ibid.

94 Scott, J., Brown, F. and Rogers, A. (2023) *Local elections 2023: Labour overtakes Conservatives as largest party of local government.* Available at: news.sky.com/story/local-elections-2023-tories-lose-control-of-three-councils-as-labour-gains-key-authority-and-wins-mayoral-race-in-early-results-12873352#:~:-text=Labour%20has%20now%20become%20the,six%20switching%20directly%20to%20Labour. (Accessed: 26 July 2023).

95 Smulian, M. (2023) *Tories make gains as Labour loses control in Slough.* Available at: lgcplus.com/politics/governance-and-structure/tories-make-gains-as-labour-loses-control-in-slough-05-05-2023 (Accessed: 26 July 2023).

England

Leaders of local councils were encouraged by the government to adopt the IHRA definition of antisemitism (along with working examples) in 2019, and prior to that in 2016. This research demonstrates that government endorsement appears to have made a tangible difference to uptake. More than half of English councils who responded to FoI requests confirmed they had adopted the IHRA definition. The government confirms at least three quarters of local councils in England have adopted; the majority that have not are surprisingly reported to be Conservative-led councils, and this is consistent with the research findings.[96] The antisemitism scandal in the Labour Party under Jeremy Corbyn's leadership may be a factor in the subsequent adoption of the IHRA definition by Labour-led councils.[97]

A total of 52 councils in England who responded confirmed that they have passed a motion to adopt the APPG Islamophobia definition. This equates to 15.6 per cent of councils in England. Of the 52 councils, the majority (34) are Labour-led councils, with nine councils having NOC, five being run by Liberal Democrats, and four being Conservative-led. The political constitution of the adopting councils is by no means surprising, with 65 per cent being Labour-controlled. Indeed, it is reflective of the national picture. The Labour Party see themselves as championing the rights of Black Asian and Minority Ethnic minority[98] (BAME) groups. (Although BAME, a vacuous and vague term, is something the government rightly committed to no longer use as of last year.)[99] Prominent Labour politicians, such as Diane Abbott, have spoken out on Islamophobia, having previously tabled an early day motion (EDM) on 'global Islamophobia' back in 2020,[100] as has the party's deputy leader Angela Rayner, who in March 2023 tweeted:

> *'Tonight I attended a reception to mark the UN's first International Day to Combat Islamophobia. It's vital that, together, we raise awareness of Islamophobia and tackle hate crimes against Muslim communities in the UK and across the world.'*[101]

At the time of writing, the tweet received over 238,000 impressions.

Table 1. 52 councils who have adopted the APPG definition as well as the IHRA definition

	APPG	Vote	IHRA	Minutes	% Muslim	Party
London Borough of Barking and Dagenham	Yes	Yes	Yes	Yes	24.4	LAB
Metropolitan Borough of Barnsley	Yes	Yes	Yes	Yes	0.6	LAB
Borough of Basildon	Yes	N/A	Yes	N/A	1.8	CON
Birmingham	Yes	N/A	Yes	Yes	29.9	LAB
Blackburn with Darwen	Yes	N/A	Yes	Yes	35	LAB
London Borough of Brent	Yes	N/A	Yes	Yes	21.4	LAB
Bristol	Yes	Yes	Yes	Yes	6.7	NOC
Calderdale	Yes	N/A	Yes	Yes	9.5	LAB

96 Harpin, L. (2021) '60 percent of councils yet to adopt IHRA are CONSERVATIVE', *Jewish News*, 15 September. Available at: jewishnews.co.uk/60-percent-of-councils-yet-to-approve-ihra-are-tory (Accessed: 26 July 2023).

97 Sabbagh, D. (2018) 'Labour adopts IHRA antisemitism definition in full', *The Guardian*, 4 September. Available at: theguardian.com/politics/2018/sep/04/labour-adopts-ihra-antisemitism-definition-in-full (Accessed: 26 July 2023).

98 Labour Party, *BAME Communities*. Available at: labour.org.uk/members/take-part/bame-communities (Accessed: 26 July 2023).

99 Laux, R. and Nisar, S. (2022) *Why we've stopped using the term 'BAME' in government*. Available at: civilservice.blog.gov.uk/2022/05/19/why-weve-stopped-using-the-term-bame-in-government (Accessed: 26 July 2023).

100 UK Parliament (2020) 'Global Islamophobia', *EDM 1164*, 18 November. Available at: edm.parliament.uk/early-day-motion/57744/global-islamophobia (Accessed: 26 July 2023).

101 Rayner, A. (2023) [Twitter] 15 March. Available at: twitter.com/AngelaRayner/status/1636106964424876032?lang=en (Accessed: 26 July 2023).

	APPG	Vote	IHRA	Minutes	% Muslim	Party
London Borough of Camden	Yes	Yes	Yes	Yes	16.1	LAB
Cheshire East	Yes	N/A	Yes	Yes	1	NOC
Chesterfield	Yes	Yes	Yes	N/A	0.9	LAB
Coventry	Yes	No	Yes	Yes	10.4	LAB
Croydon	Yes	Yes	Yes	Yes	10.4	NOC
Metropolitan Borough of Doncaster	Yes	No	Yes	Yes	2.2	LAB
London Borough of Ealing	Yes	N/A	Yes	Yes	18.8	LAB
London Borough of Enfield	Yes	Yes	Yes	Yes	18.6	LAB
London Borough of Hackney	Yes	Yes	Yes	Yes	13.3	LAB
London Borough of Haringey	Yes	Yes	Yes	Yes	12.6	LAB
Harlow	Yes	Yes	Yes	Yes	4	NOC
London Borough of Harrow	Yes	Yes	Yes	Yes	15.9	CON
Hyndburn	Yes	N/A	Yes	Yes	14.7	NOC
Ipswich	Yes	N/A	Yes	Yes	3.9	LAB
London Borough of Islington	Yes	N/A	No*	Yes	11.9	LAB
Kingston upon Hull	Yes	Yes	Yes	Yes	3.5	LIB DEM
Kirklees	Yes	N/A	Yes	Yes	18.5	LAB
Knowsley	Yes	Yes	Yes	Yes	0.6	LAB
London Borough of Lambeth	Yes	N/A	Yes	Yes	8.1	LAB
Leicester	Yes	N/A	Yes	Yes	23.5	LAB
London Borough of Lewisham	Yes	Yes	Yes	Yes	7.4	LAB
Manchester	Yes	N/A	Yes	N/A	22.3	LAB
Newcastle upon Tyne	Yes	Yes	Yes	Yes	9	LAB
London Borough of Newham	Yes	N/A	Yes	Yes	34.8	LAB
Metropolitan Borough of Oldham	Yes	Yes	Yes	Yes	24.4	LAB
Peterborough	Yes	Yes	Yes	Yes	12.2	NOC
London Borough of Redbridge	Yes	Yes	Yes	Yes	31.3	LAB
London Borough of Richmond upon Thames	Yes	Yes	Yes	Yes	4.3	LIB DEM
City of Salford	Yes	N/A	Yes	Yes	5	LAB
Sefton	Yes	Yes	Yes	Yes	0.8	LAB
Sheffield	Yes	N/A	Yes	Yes	10.3	NOC
South Kesteven	Yes	N/A	Yes	Yes	0.5	CON
South Oxfordshire	Yes	Yes	Yes	Yes	1	NOC
London Borough of Southwark	Yes	N/A	Yes	Yes	9.6	LAB
Stroud	Yes	Yes	Yes	Yes	0.3	NOC
Telford and Wrekin	Yes	N/A	Yes	Yes	2.7	LAB
Three Rivers District	Yes	Yes	Yes	Yes	3.7	LIB DEM

	APPG	Vote	IHRA	Minutes	% Muslim	Party
London Borough of Tower Hamlets	Yes	Yes	Yes	Yes	39.9	LAB
Vale of White Horse	Yes	N/A	Yes	Yes	1.4	LIB DEM
City of Wakefield	Yes	Yes	Yes	Yes	3.2	LAB
Metropolitan Borough of Walsall	Yes	N/A	Yes	N/A	11.3	CON
London Borough of Waltham Forest	Yes	Yes	Yes	Yes	21.6	LAB
Watford	Yes	Yes	Yes	Yes	13	LIB DEM
Wolverhampton	Yes	Yes	Yes	Yes	5.5	LAB

*Source: FoI. Note: Islington Council has not formally adopted the IHRA definition, however they have published a statement on their website, titled 'Countering antisemitism in the workplace', which makes passing reference to it.

Responding to a tweet from Anneliese Dodds on Home Office statistics pointing to the 42 per cent of all victims of perceived religious hate crime being Muslim, the Labour leader Starmer tweeted, 'We must do everything we can to ensure we eradicate Islamophobia in our society'.[102] Dodds's tweet also said, 'Labour has adopted the APPG on British Muslims' definition of Islamophobia. It's time the Conservatives followed suit.'[103] The fact that a senior political figure's tweet fails to acknowledge legitimate concerns around the APPG definition, equality before the law and free speech, not least the implications it may have on counterterror efforts, speaks volumes.

On referrals to the government's counterextremism programme Prevent, the Shawcross review emphasises:

> *'[F]ears of being accused of being racist, anti-Muslim, or culturally-insensitive may inhibit Islamist-related referrals in a way that that does not appear to be the case for other types of ideological concern'.*[104]

The Labour party published an *Islamophobia Complaints Handbook* which has a foreword from Dodds. The document states:

> *'The Labour Party adopted the APPG definition and its examples in March 2019 as an important statement of principle, solidarity and legitimacy. The Labour Party's governing body and administrative authority, the National Executive Committee (the NEC) reaffirmed that position in 2021 when it adopted the Labour Party's Code of Conduct on Islamophobia.'*[105]

As previously discussed, both the Labour Party, Scottish Labour, the (Labour) London Mayor's office and the Liberal Democrats adopted the definition, whilst the Conservative government rejected it. Notably, the research shows that several councils chose to adopt the APPG and IHRA definition at the same time, with some motions put forward – for example, the London Borough of Ealing – combining both. A parallel trend is observed in one case in Wales, but not in Scotland, although East Ayrshire Council has adopted the APPG definition, but surprisingly not the government-backed IHRA. The same scenario occurred in the London Borough of Islington – where Corbyn is the sitting Member of Parliament. Islington council however confirmed they have a statement on antisemitism published on their intranet. The statement is titled 'Countering antisemitism in the workplace' and does refer to the IHRA definition. However, a story in the *Jewish Chronicle* in August 2020 highlights Corbyn's local Labour Party put forward a motion to reject the internationally recognised definition of antisemitism.[106] One of the reasons for objection expressed in the motion being the alleged conflation of anti-Zionism with antisemitism.[107]

102 Starmer, K. (2021) [Twitter] 2 November. Available at: twitter.com/Keir_Starmer/status/1455581171140726793?s=20 (Accessed: 26 July 2023).

103 Dodds, A. (2021) [Twitter] 1 November. Available at: twitter.com/AnnelieseDodds/status/1455148842089947146?s=20 (Accessed: 26 July 2023).

104 Home Office (2019) *Independent Review of Prevent*. Available at: gov.uk/government/collections/independent-review-of-prevent (Accessed: 26 July 2023).

105 Labour Party (2023) *Islamophobia Complaints Handbook*. Available at: labour.org.uk (Accessed: 26 July 2023).

106 Harpin, L. (2020) 'Corbyn's CLP to debate rejecting international definition of antisemitism', *Jewish Chronicle*, 3 August. Available at: thejc.com/news/uk/corbyn-s-islington-north-clp-to-debate-rejecting-international-definition-of-antisemitism-1.502223 (Accessed: 26 July 2023).

107 Ibid.

As part of the data collection, the percentage Muslim population (obtained from the 2021 census data) for each LA in England and Wales was collated to see if any patterns emerged where councils had adopted the APPG definition. Was there, for example, consistently more adoption where the Muslim population was greater? Do local authorities with smaller Muslim populations still adopt? The following LA areas who have adopted the definition indeed have significant Muslim populations (percentage population highlighted in brackets after each respective LA): London Borough of Waltham Forest (21.6 per cent), London Borough of Tower Hamlets (39.9 per cent), London Borough of Redbridge (31.3 per cent), London Borough of Brent (21.4 per cent), London Borough of Barking and Dagenham (24.4 per cent), London Borough of Newham (34.8 per cent), Metropolitan Borough of Oldham (24.4 per cent), Manchester (22.3 per cent), Blackburn with Darwen (35 per cent) and Birmingham (29.9 per cent).

Other local authorities, which have comparatively much smaller Muslim populations, have also adopted. For example, the Metropolitan Borough of Barnsley (0.6 per cent), Cheshire East (one per cent), Chesterfield (0.9 per cent), Knowsley (0.6 per cent), South Kesteven (0.5 per cent) and London Borough of Richmond upon Thames (4.3 per cent). Therefore, there does not appear to be a clear pattern indicating adoption in areas only with sizeable Muslim populations, although the average Muslim population for the 52 councils in question equates to 11.8 per cent – which is more than one in 10 people. Notably, there are also a significant number of councils (150) who have not adopted the APPG definition where the Muslim population is under five per cent according to the research findings. There are also 40 councils where the population is over five per cent, and where there has been no adoption.

Notably, the London Borough of Islington was one of the first to adopt the APPG definition – the minutes from a meeting in February 2019, note:

> *'The terrorist attack committed by Darren Osbourne outside Muslim Welfare House affected the whole community, but it was Muslims who were the specific target of that attack. The Leader was proud of how Islington's communities came together in the hours and days after the attack and rallied round to make it clear that Islington was welcoming to all. By adopting this definition, the Council was putting on record that it would not stand for anti-Muslim hatred.'*

Notably, 'anti-Muslim hatred' is used interchangeably with Islamophobia. Perhaps a distinction should be drawn between the exercise of adopting the definition, versus the realities of countering anti-Muslim prejudice? Does the former influence the latter? A press release on the APPG adoption issued on 1 March 2019, titled 'Islington council takes a stand against Islamophobia', quotes both the council leader, Richard Watts, as well as the Chair of Finsbury Park Mosque, Mohammed Kozbar.

Harlow council adopted the APPG definition in January 2020, but one of the working examples appears to be redacted. It is not clear whether this is an erroneous omission, or a deliberate choice. Harlow cite the working example, 'Using the symbols and images associated with classic Islamophobia', however in the APPG report *Islamophobia Defined*, the full version of this working example reads:

> *'Using the symbols and images associated with classic Islamophobia (e.g. Muhammed being a paedophile, claims of Muslims spreading Islam by the sword or subjugating minority groups under their rule) to characterize Muslims as being 'sex groomers', inherently violent or incapable of living harmoniously in plural societies.'*[108]

On 'sex groomers' – provocative anti-Muslim chants[109] of far-right groups like Britain First must be condemned in the strongest possible terms. However, the Home Secretary Suella Braverman faced significant backlash for highlighting the disproportionate representation of Pakistani heritage men (as evidenced in inquiries

108 All Party Parliamentary Group on British Muslims, *Islamophobia defined*. Available at: static1.squarespace.com/static/599c3d2febbd1a90cffdd8a9/t/5bfd1ea3352f531a6170ceee/1543315109493/Islamophobia+Defined.pdf (Accessed: 26 July 2023).

109 Jones, S. (2017) 'Far right Britain First marchers chant 'Muslim paedos off our streets' parading through Rochdale', *Daily Mirror*, 22 July. Available at: mirror.co.uk/news/uk-news/britain-first-marchers-chant-muslim-10854763 (Accessed: 26 July 2023).

into Rotherham,[110] Telford,[111] and Rochdale)[112] in sexual 'grooming gang' cases.[113] She later told the National Conservatism conference:

> '*...the ethnicity of grooming gang perpetrators is the sort of fact that has become unfashionable in some quarters. Much like the fact that 100 percent of women do not have a penis.*'[114]

There is danger this working example could further stymie[115] free discussion on this, a matter of significant public interest and a scandal described as a 'nation's shame'.[116] Several council areas, which have been impacted by 'grooming gangs', have adopted the APPG definition, like Telford and Wrekin,[117] Wakefield and Manchester.

Salford council is another council which didn't use the full version of the working example, as observed in the minutes of a meeting dated 15 July 2020.[118]

The London Borough of Tower Hamlets adopted the definition, as recorded in the council minutes dated 20 March 2019. The minutes note, 'bearded men attacked for the personification of a Muslim identity or even turban wearing Sikhs attacked due to the perception of Muslimness.' The minutes fail to note that many cases of 'mistaken identity' incidents targeting Sikhs, or white non-Muslim hipsters (who often have long beards) for that matter,[119] are in relation to conflation of their identity, with that of extremists Muslims – like the Taliban, Osama bin Laden or Islamic State. So, there appears to be no distinction between the 'Muslimness' of violent jihadists, and that of ordinary law-abiding British Muslims. White non-Muslim hipsters aren't targeted because of their race, so to suggest targeting of them is a 'type of racism' is flawed, as equally would be the case for white Sikh converts.

The working example edited by Harlow and Salford omits sentences which include, 'claims of Muslims spreading Islam by the sword or subjugating minority groups under their rule'. On the face of it, the original version of this specific working example appears to seek censorship of historical facts and truths. The BBC appear to agree with this principle, given their attempted censorship (for fear of offending Muslims) of Lord Singh of Wimbledon on Radio 4's *Thought for the Day* in 2019, when he wanted to talk about the martyrdom of the ninth Sikh Guru. Guru Tegh Bahadur was beheaded for standing up for the freedom of religion of Kashmiri Hindus being forced to convert to Islam, 'by the sword' by the then Mughal ruler Aurangzeb.[120] There are of course some positive aspects to Ottoman, Mughal, and Moorish rule, but to suggest Islam wasn't spread by such conquering empires through the sword is frankly false, mischievous and a form of historical revisionism. These important particulars aren't likely to have been carefully scrutinised or discussed prior to 'unanimous' adoption by local councils up and down the country. But councils who've adopted might now want to give their

110 Jay, A. (2014) *Independent Inquiry into Child Sexual Exploitation in Rotherham*, Rotherham Metropolitan Borough Council. Available at: rotherham.gov.uk (Accessed: 26 July 2023).

111 Independent Inquiry into Telford Child Sexual Exploitation. Available at: iitcse.com (Accessed: 26 July 2023).

112 greatermanchester-ca.gov.uk/media/2569/operation_augusta_january_2020_digital_final.pdf

113 The Home Secretary said, 'What's clear is that what we've seen is a practice whereby vulnerable white English girls, sometimes in care, sometimes who are in challenging circumstances, being pursued and raped and drugged and harmed by gangs of British Pakistani men who've worked in child abuse rings or networks.' Brown, F. (2023) *Suella Braverman describes grooming gang comments as 'unfashionable facts' after backlash*. Available at: news.sky.com/story/suella-braverman-describes-grooming-gang-comments-as-unfashionable-facts-after-backlash-12861676 (Accessed: 26 July 2023).

114 Spyro, S. (2023) 'NO woman has a penis – Suella Braverman hits back at 'fashionable fictions'', *Daily Express*, 15 May. Available at: express.co.uk/news/politics/1770591/women-penis-suella-braverman (Accessed: 26 July 2023).

115 The Independent Inquiry into Telford Child Exploitation revealed more than 1,000 girls had been abused over a 40-year period, and that agencies blamed victims for the abuse they suffered, not the perpetrators, and some cases of exploitation were not investigated because of 'nervousness about race'.

116 *The Times* (2012) 'A nation's shame: hundreds of girls sexually abused by networks of men', 9 May. Available at: thetimes.co.uk/article/a-nations-shame-hundreds-of-girls-sexually-abused-by-networks-of-men-3wwwf3gdvb7 (Accessed: 26 July 2023).

117 Tom Crowther QC who headed up the Independent Inquiry – Telford Child Sexual Exploitation, said that the failure of the authorities to intervene was in part driven by 'a nervousness that investigating concerns against Asian men, in particular, would inflame racial tensions'. The inquiry revealed that 1,000 mainly white girls had been subjected to horrific sexual abuse by groups of men of mainly Pakistani heritage since at least the 1980s. Telford and Wrekin council adopted the full version of the working example which refers to 'sex groomers' as outlined in their Equality and Diversity update dated 7 October 2021 (obtained under FoI).

118 In May 2023, @salfordCouncil Twitter account posted an image of its employees taking the knee as a gesture of solidarity with George Floyd on the third anniversary of his death, along with the words, 'we will continue to push for a more inclusive society for all'.

119 Bullen, J. (2015) 'Swedish bearded men mistaken for Isis terrorists after waving black flag during photocall', *Evening Standard*, 12 October. Available at: standard.co.uk/news/world/swedish-bearded-men-mistaken-for-isis-terrorists-after-waving-black-flag-during-photocall-a3088626.html (Accessed: 26 July 2023).

120 Kennedy, D. (2019) 'Swedish bearded men mistaken for Isis terrorists after waving black flag during photocall', *The Times*, 4 October. Available at: thetimes.co.uk/article/sikh-peer-leaves-bbc-radio-4-show-with-swipe-at-thought-police-m3vcjg77w (Accessed: 26 July 2023).

employees reassurances that they can talk freely about history or religion without being deemed 'racists', since Islamophobia is 'a type of racism' according to the definition adopted.[121]

But there is little optimism on the horizon when considering an example where the APPG definition has not in fact been adopted. In May 2023 it was reported that one councillor from Boston Council, who was scheduled to be appointed Mayor, was denied the role for Facebook posts made in 2022, which were alleged to constitute 'hateful speech' towards Muslims. The 'offending' posts were made during the 2022 Qatar World Cup and were in relation to Islam.[122] The councillor raised concerns about aspects of Islamic doctrine which criminalise homosexuality and severely restrict the rights of women in Qatar. Most ordinary people would agree these statements are fair comment, and he had some support amongst colleagues. However, another councillor said he was denied the Mayoralty due to social media posts that people 'just couldn't accept' with phrases that people found 'offensive.'[123] This example demonstrates how legitimate criticism of specific aspects of questionable doctrine, which is bigoted towards certain groups, is perversely considered 'hateful' in itself.

There have been different outcomes on APPG adoption elsewhere. Indeed, where opposition voices have been heard, some councils, like Aberdeenshire, voted instead for a motion to 'note' the definition, rather than formal adoption itself. This decision was influenced by the lobbying efforts of the National Secular Society (NSS). Its chief executive Stephen Evans had warned the definition, 'might be a counterproductive way of addressing anti-Muslim bigotry and hatred.' The motion to 'note' the Islamophobia definition included a commitment to 'condemn all discrimination against race or belief', which is a more inclusive approach. However, the Aberdeenshire decision sparked some local controversy – the council were accused of putting forward 'flimsy accuses'[124] not to adopt, by a Muslim councillor. Far from being 'flimsy', the decision was based on a comprehensive review, outlining evidence both for and against adoption of the said definition. It is the opinion of the author that amongst the significant volume of documents obtained and considered for this research, the process of review in Aberdeenshire is an exemplar.

A report (on the 17 November 2022) to the Business Services Committee on the definition includes consideration of 'negative consequences' of adopting, along with reasons to consider adoption. A 'key concerns' section making reference to the Civitas open letter to the Home Secretary, as well as the Policy Exchange report *On Islamophobia The Problem of Definition*.[125] Whilst flagging the negative, the authors also made reference to the council receiving an open letter from Muslim Engagement and Development (MEND) from February 2022, urging all Scottish councils to adopt the definition, along with accompanying guidelines from a group called the Coalition Against Islamophobia. Most notably, in one section (3.6.4) the authors, point out: 'the report questions the necessity of the definition when considered alongside the protections for protected characteristics enshrined in the Equality Act 2010.'

The NSS's Chief Executive Officer, Stephen Evans, shared the following commentary on their ongoing pushback against the definition, titled 'Resisting the Islamophobia definition'.

121 This presents the absurd situation where you can talk freely about the crusades without being labelled a 'Christianophobe' but may think twice before discussing jihads.

122 National Secular Society (2023) *NSS warns council on free speech after 'Islamophobia' allegations*. Available at: secularism.org.uk/news/2023/05/nss-warns-council-on-free-speech-after-islamophobia-allegations (Accessed: 26 July 2023).

123 Ibid.

124 Topp, K. (2022) *Aberdeenshire Council accused of 'flimsy excuses' in Islamophobia debate*. Available at: pressandjournal.co.uk/fp/news/aberdeen-aberdeenshire/5058835/aberdeenshire-council-islamophobia (Accessed: 26 July 2023).

125 Phillips, T., Jenkins, J. and Frampton, M. (2019) *On Islamophobia: The Problem of Definition*, Policy Exchange. Available at: policyexchange.org.uk (Accessed: 26 July 2023).

Resisting the Islamophobia definition

'The right to speak freely about religion is an issue close to our hearts at the National Secular Society. A former NSS president George W Foote was once jailed for publishing 'blasphemous' cartoons. As an organisation we've gone from being prosecuted for blasphemy to being instrumental in the abolition of the blasphemy laws, in 2008. Our conception of secularism includes the conviction that criticism of ideologies and beliefs is important and necessary. After campaigning so vigorously to see Britain's blasphemy laws abolished, we are determined to ensure that new de-facto blasphemy laws aren't introduced by the back door.

'The All-Party Parliamentary Group on British Muslims define Islamophobia as 'a type of racism that targets expressions of Muslimness or perceived Muslimness'.

'Our central concern with APPG definition, and the term Islamophobia itself, is the way in which it conflates criticism of Islam or Islamic practices with hatred of Muslims. In a liberal secular society, individuals should be afforded respect and protection, but ideas should not. In our view, the adoption of this definition has the potential to chill freedom of expression, including academic and journalistic freedom.

'In 2018 we responded to the APPG's call for evidence on a 'Working definition of Islamophobia/Anti-Muslim hatred' to caution against use of the term 'Islamophobia', arguing that a distinction needed to be drawn between anti-Muslim bigotry and hatred, directed against individuals or Muslims as a whole, and criticism of Islamic ideas, ideology, or practices. The concept of Islamophobia and the proposed definition categorically fails to make this distinction.

'Nevertheless, the APPG stuck with the contested term. At the launch of the APPG report, Sayeeda Warsi, a prominent member of the APPG, acknowledged concerns over the term but said she was prepared to go along with it because the Muslim 'community' preferred it.[126]

'Attempts to limit speech critical of Islam is nothing new. Between 1999 and 2010, a coalition of 57 Islamic nations known as the Organisation of Islamic Cooperation (OIC) pushed 'defamation of religion' resolutions at the United Nations. Proponents argued that Muslims were facing growing intolerance and discrimination, which they described as 'Islamophobia'. But human rights and secularist groups warned that the focus on protecting Islam rather than individuals amounted to an attempt to impose a global blasphemy law.

'The campaign by the Islamic nations faced opposition from western democracies, which argued that the 'defamation of religion' resolutions would violate the right to freedom of speech, thought, conscience and religion. Eventually the 'defamation' approach was abandoned.

'Attempts to define Islamophobia as a form of racism pose a similar problem. Because the term 'expressions of Muslimness' can be taken to mean Islamic practices generally, the Islamophobia definition clearly risks criticisms of a particular religious practice being characterised as a 'form or racism' or 'hateful'.

'In a society which is free and democratic, religious beliefs and practices must remain open to scrutiny and debate. Adoption of this definition opens the door to allegations of Islamophobia being used to effectively shield Islam and even Islamic extremists from criticism. Legitimate criticisms or concerns about Islamic practices risk being judged beyond the bounds of reasonable public debate. Those that transgress the imposed limits will be censured. Those wishing to avoid allegations of racism may choose to self-censor. It is in this way that free speech is stifled.

126 Sloggart, C. (2018) *The gatekeepers of public debate can't patronise away anti-Muslim bigotry*. Available at: secularism.org.uk/opinion/2018/11/the-gate-keepers-of-public-debate-cant-patronise-away-anti-muslim-bigotry (Accessed: 26 July 2023).

'Nevertheless, within months of the APPG on British Muslims 'Islamophobia Defined' report being published, the Labour party, Liberal Democrats, Plaid Cymru, the mayor of London and all five major political parties in Scotland were among those to have adopted the definition.

'Concerned with the way in which this vague definition was being hastily adopted without adequate scrutiny or proper consideration of its potential harms, we joined others in urging against its adoption.

'A letter we co-ordinated from secularist organisations to the then home secretary Sajid Javid urging him not to adopt the definition was swiftly followed by an open letter from a more diverse range of 44 campaigners, academics, writers, and other public figures. These included the NSS, representatives of Civitas, the Council of Ex-Muslims of Britain, the Network of Sikh Organisations, Christian Concern, and individuals including Richard Dawkins and Peter Tatchell – all arguing that the definition was 'unfit for purpose'.

'Our first significant success came when the government rejected the definition. Whist insisting that hatred directed against Muslims and others because of their faith or heritage was 'utterly unacceptable', it said the wording needed 'further careful consideration', had 'not been broadly accepted' and would have 'severe consequences for freedom of speech'.

'The government later cautioned that the term Islamophobia has been used to shut down debate. Speaking during a House of Lords debate in November 2021, Stephen Greenhalgh, the then minister of state at the Department for Levelling Up, Housing and Communities, said Islamophobia has been used as a 'heckler's veto to shut down alternative opinions'.

'Nevertheless, many local authorities continued to adopt the definition in response to lobbying from the APPG on British Muslims and allied groups such as MEND. The definition has been adopted with the best of intentions – or as one local council put it: 'to demonstrate the local authority's commitment to supporting the Muslim community' – but with insufficient scrutiny.

'We have therefore adopted the strategy of briefing local councillors ahead of any decision to adopt, to at least ensure that councils are aware of the potential negative consequences.

'This strategy bore fruit when Lancashire County Council became the first local authority to reject the proposed definition in 2019 following NSS lobbying.

'Then, in 2022, Aberdeenshire Council voted not to adopt the 'Islamophobia' definition after we were invited to address their meeting. We urged the council to find other ways to foster social cohesion and of tackling anti-Muslim hatred that don't conflate race with religion or the criticism of ideas with hostility against people. Following our intervention, councillors voted to instead 'note the definition of Islamophobia', 'condemn all discrimination against race or belief', and 'agree to address any anti-Muslim bias or prejudice identified in Aberdeenshire'.

'These councillors should be commended for applying some healthy scepticism to the definition and the concept of Islamophobia. The decision to note the definition, rather than adopt it, while working to end anti-Muslim discrimination and bigotry strikes a reasonable balance between protecting people from harm and protecting the fundamental right to free speech. We hope other councils take note of this approach.

'As one of the Aberdeenshire councillors remarked during the debate, the widespread adoption of the Islamophobia definition is part of a 'tide of little erosions' of which the overall effect is a 'dilution of one of our most precious values.' We will continue to play our part in holding back the tide.'

Multiple Islamophobia definitions have been adopted by local authorities in England

Whilst the research findings show a single definition of antisemitism has been adopted by local authorities, the most remarkable finding is the existence of panoply of definitions of 'Islamophobia'/'anti-Muslim' hatred being adopted by councils across England.

Whilst a minority (52 out of 318) have endorsed the APPG definition, several councils have instead chosen to opt for an alternative definition. Some have based this decision on stressing the importance of formulating their own, following discussion and dialogue with members of the local Muslim community, like the London Borough of Barnet and Bradford. This consultative approach demonstrates an attempt at grass roots community engagement. Part of the decision making in Bradford was related to concerns about the word 'Muslimness'. Other councils have chosen to adopt alternative Islamophobia definitions, like the Runnymede Trust version from their 2017 report *Islamophobia – 20 years on, still a challenge for us all*,[127] or the MEND definition.

According to the 2021 census, 33.4 per cent of people in Bradford described themselves as Christian, while 30.5 per cent described themselves as Muslim.[128] In 10 years, there has been a significant change in the religious profile of the Yorkshire city. Bradford District Council set up a 'Joint Islamophobia Definition Working Group' and consulted a variety of stakeholders, including academics, imams, and religious scholars, to formulate 'the Bradford definition'. The group was convened by Councillor Abdul Jabar, and included Bradford Hate Crime Alliance and the Bradford Council for Mosques. The council adopted its own definition with local consultation, as it stated 'Muslimness' in the APPG definition was 'unclear to its meaning'.

'Islamophobia is a direct or indirect act(s) of hatred and discrimination against people (individuals or groups) of Islamic faith on grounds of their belief and practice' – **'The Bradford definition'.**

Source: Bradford council meeting minutes, 16 July 2019 – obtained via FoI.

The London Borough of Barnet also chose to consult their local Muslim community to come up with a definition of Islamophobia. The previous administration rejected the APPG definition, so in 2019 a cross-party motion agreed a definition, 'should be developed through consultation with Barnet's Muslim communities.' In line with the Bradford's consultative approach, workshops were held with a forum of Islamic organisations from across the borough and included students from Barnet Hill Academy.

The Islamophobia/anti-Muslim prejudice definition below was unanimously voted for adoption at a full council in October 2002:

'Anti-Muslim prejudice, also known as islamophobia, is a perception of Muslims, often expressed as a dislike or hatred towards an individual, a group or their property, institutions and facilities for possessing the perceived characteristics of a Muslim. This prejudice is often rooted in racism, and can be manifested in many ways, including but not limited to abusive behaviour, threats of violence, damage and desecration of property, assault and extreme violence' – **Barnet Council, 'anti-Muslim prejudice/ Islamophobia' definition.**

Source: Barnet Council FoI response, which quotes the Barnet definition from council meeting minutes of 20 October 2020.

127 Elahi, F. and Khan, O. (2017) *Islamophobia: Still A Challenge For Us All, Runnymede Trust.* Available at: runnymedetrust.org (Accessed: 26 July 2023).

128 ONS (2023) *How life has changed in Bradford: Census 2021.* Available at: ons.gov.uk/visualisations/censusareachanges/E08000032 (Accessed: 26 July 2023).

In October 2019, The London Borough of Hounslow adopted the European Commission against Racism and Intolerance (ECRI) definition of Islamophobia instead. The official record states that in resolving to adopt the ECRI definition the council 'reiterate our commitment to opposing anti-semitism [sic] and to campaign against all forms of racism.' This statement appears to support the contested APPG idea that Islamophobia is a form of racism.

'Islamophobia is a contrived fear or prejudice fomented by the existing Eurocentric and Orientalist global power structure. It is directed at a perceived or real Muslim threat through the maintenance and extension of existing disparities in economic, political, social and cultural relations, while rationalizing the necessity to deploy violence as a tool to achieve 'civilizational rehab' of the target communities (Muslim or otherwise). Islamophobia reintroduces and reaffirms a global racial structure through which resource distribution disparities are maintained and extended' – **Hounslow council adopted (ECRI) definition of Islamophobia.**

Source: Hounslow Council meeting minutes, 29 October 2019 – obtained via FoI.

Runnymede Borough Council confirmed their definition of Islamophobia was taken from the Runnymede Trust 20th Anniversary Report. It was incorporated into 'The Equality Policy', which was agreed by the council in March 2021.

'Islamophobia is any distinction, exclusion, or restriction towards, or preference against, Muslims (or those perceived to be Muslims) that has the purpose or effect of nullifying or impairing the recognition, enjoyment or exercise, on an equal footing, of human rights and fundamental freedoms in the political, economic, social, cultural or any other field of public life' – **Runnymede Borough Council adopted the Runnymede Trust definition of Islamophobia, 20th Anniversary Report.**

Source: Runnymede Borough Council Corporate Management Committee meeting minutes, 25 February 2021 – obtained via FoI.

Slough Borough Council adopted the MEND definition of Islamophobia in July 2019.

'Islamophobia is a prejudice, aversion, hostility, or hatred towards Muslims and encompasses any distinction, exclusion, restriction, discrimination, or preference against Muslims that has the purpose or effect of nullifying or impairing the recognition, enjoyment or exercise, on an equal footing, of human rights and fundamental freedoms in the political, economic, social, cultural or any other field of public life' **– Slough Borough Council adopted the MEND definition of Islamophobia.**

Source: Slough Borough Council meeting minutes, 23 July 2019 – obtained via FoI.

Notably, the MEND definition does not appear to conflate religion with race. The APPG one is a concern for freedom of speech, given it risks drawing in criticism of Islam. But this definition is for the total inclusion of Islamic religious choices, irrespective of whether others agree with them, or not.

The process of 'adoption' of motions is the political mechanism by which councils in England, Wales and Scotland have endorsed the APPG Islamophobia definition. The passing (or approval) of motions is 'voted' for, which is usually indicative of a raising of hands in the council chamber, as opposed to a formal vote. Voting is not always recorded, however there is normally a record if a motion is passed or not. Kirklees, for example confirm, 'it wasn't a recorded vote, but the definition was adopted in the resolution'. Often the decision is described as 'unanimously' passed. However, there is the odd occasion when specific voting decisions are in fact recorded, and a breakdown provided for those who voted in 'favour', 'against' or 'abstained' from the motion put forward.

In Peterborough, for example, the motion to adopt the APPG definition was put forward by one councillor, however was contested, with free speech being raised as a specific objection. In the end, 31 councillors voted in favour, 22 voted against, and six abstained from voting. The motion was seconded by another councillor, but it was highlighted that the APPG definition put forward in the motion 'was not agreed by the National Police Chiefs Council and it was felt it would be premature to agree the wording at this stage.' Although an opposing amendment was put forward by some members outlining concerns about how the proposed definition could 'present a hinderance to free speech', it was defeated by vote.

Peterborough is not unusual in that bottom-up support or lobbying is implemented on adoption, despite central government rejection. This is a broader observable trend amongst the 52 councils who have adopted in England. Manchester's minutes note a specific action for the council on adoption:

> *'Write to government ministers asking them to listen to Muslim communities and the cross-party group of MPs and peers and to adopt this definition of Islamophobia which classifies discrimination against Muslims as a form of racism'.*

Most councils are Labour-led, with Newcastle upon Tyne minutes also capturing the following: 'Council notes MCB (Muslim Council of Britain) request to investigate [the] Conservative party' for Islamophobia. Two areas, both of which are Labour-run – Wakefield and the London Borough of Waltham Forest – refer to the lobbying efforts of the campaigning group MEND in their minutes.

The Peterborough FoI response, for example, reveals post-vote recommendations in the minutes, signally bottom-up lobbying:

> *'This Council asks the Chief Executive of the Council to:*
>
> '1. *Write to our two local members of Parliament and the Secretary of State for Levelling Up, Housing and Communities asking them to listen to Muslim communities and the cross-party group of MPs and peers and to adopt this definition of Islamophobia which classifies discrimination against Muslims as a form of racism.*
>
> '2. *Continue to prioritise tackling hate crime and Islamophobia in partnership. Peterborough City Council works with partners such as Cambridgeshire Police, on a rolling basis, and will now coordinate future actions in line with this definition of Islamophobia for all Muslims.'*
>
> Source: Peterborough City Council minutes dated 22 June 2022 – obtained via FoI.

The Metropolitan Borough of Walsall is another council where adoption of the APPG definition was contested. The motion, moved and seconded by two councillors, split the council – with 28 votes for, 24 against, two abstentions. South Oxfordshire Council minutes flagged concerns about free speech too, with both the IHRA and APPG definition adopted at the same time, however the minutes include the following free speech consideration:

> *'Council holds the right to freedom of speech and freedom of religion as fundamentals but freedom of speech is not an unlimited right, and should not be used to advocate racial or religious hatred that constitutes incitement to discrimination, hostility or violence.'*

The stated caveat around the limit to free speech is consistent with the law. In July 2019 the London Borough of Hillingdon carried an alternative motion rather than one proposed to adopt the APPG definition. It reads:

> *'[T]hat this Council expresses alarm at the rise in Islamophobia in recent years across the UK. This includes incidents where Muslim men and women have been physically assaulted, Mosques have been set on fire and Muslim figures have faced disproportionate online abuse.'*

The motion went on to recognise the 'robust equalities policies' the council has in place to ensure 'fair and equitable' treatment of all its residents. It did, however, ask the Cabinet to consider the APPG recommendations, as part of the ongoing review of equality policies.

On adoption of the APPG definition, the minutes of Birmingham City Council emphasise:

> *'The best way to tackle all types of hate is through education. The No Outsiders Programme developed in this City and other similar education programmes used in schools have an essential role to play in ending discrimination against all protected groups under the Equalities Act 2010 and as such should be given this Council's full support.'*

Note both the latter two examples emphasise the LA commitment to all groups under equality law.

The Equality Act 2010 and Public Sector Equality Duty

Councils are committed to tackle discrimination of protected characteristics and advancing equality of opportunity and promoting good relations for both their employees and the local community, through the Equality and Diversity Framework 2021-2025. This aims to ensure compliance with the Public Sector Equality Duty established by the Equality Act 2010. The Local Government Association have an 'Understanding equality' section on their website which reads:

> *'The Equality Act 2010 challenges organisations to know how age, disability, gender reassignment, marriage and civil partnership, pregnancy and maternity, race, religion/belief, sex, and sexual orientation describe the experiences of local communities, both individually and collectively. Thinking about the relationship between these 'protected characteristics' explains the difficulties and opportunities arising from the diversity of local areas. They are a reminder that the consequences of difference on effective service delivery cannot be avoided either for the provider or the user.'*[129]

They go on, 'Organisations are expected to use this understanding to demonstrate 'due regard' to the Public Sector Equality Duty to':

1. Eliminate unlawful discrimination, harassment and victimisation and other conduct prohibited by the act;
2. Advance equality of opportunity between people who share a protected characteristic and those who do not; and
3. Foster good relations between people who share a protected characteristic and those who do not.

It is not clear how LA adoption of exclusive definitions of hate crime for two faith groups serves to advance 'equality of opportunity'; rather it could be argued that the act of adoption itself serves to create a hierarchy of religions/beliefs.

To 'foster good relations', an equitable approach must surely be desirable, rather than one that promotes exclusivity and special considerations for specific groups? As we will see, this becomes a bone of contention within a Scottish council, where members raised another 'phobia' they had personally experienced during a debate on adopting the APPG definition. One could go as far as suggesting that the status quo creates an unequal, unequitable, and discriminatory environment for Christians, Hindus, Sikhs, and those of no faith – who constitute the second biggest group after Christians, according to the latest census data.

As things stand, a level playing field clearly does not exist. This, one of our key recommendations, is that local councils who have adopted the IHRA and APPG definitions, promote inclusivity with a broader equality consideration, so that one body of law applies to all, and this should be reflected to mirror existing provisions for Muslims and Jews in internal policies, delivery of services, and regularly kept under review. Embedding such considerations on a level-pegging into equalities policy should be a bare minimum requirement.

129 Local Government Association, *Equality Framework for Local Government*. Available at: local.gov.uk/our-support/guidance-and-resources/equality-frameworks/equality-framework-local-government (Accessed: 26 July 2023).

Adoption across local authorities in England

It would be too time consuming to discuss the findings from all the meeting minutes disclosed through FoI. The full disclosure included well over a thousand documents. However, for the sake of brevity, a summary of several examples in England are provided to illustrate the variety of discussion, contributions made by elected officials, and debate around how adoption of the APPG definition fits around local government's public sector equalities duties in line with the Equality Act 2010. Some of these findings could be best described as peculiar, others suggest a misunderstanding of the law and policy, whilst some demonstrate how some areas truly live up to the ultra-progressive reputation of their cities, like Bristol.

Bristol City Council – No Overall Control

Bristol City Council adopted the APPG on British Muslims definition of Islamophobia as part of a refresh to their Equality and Inclusion Policy and Strategy which was unanimously approved by Full Council on 8 December 2020. The updated policy also included the adoption of the Stonewall definition of 'Trans', recognising 'Gender Identity' and 'Gender Expression', and guidance on reducing the use of the acronym 'BAME'.

The updated policy refers to 'internal' and 'external' consultation on the APPG definition. Bristol Muslim Strategic Leadership Group (BMSLG) and Bristol Hate Crime and Discrimination Services showed support for the council to adopt the APPG definition. Although BMSLG:

> *'...added a caveat that although the definition does not completely encompass all views expressed at BMSLG (and possibly other Muslims in Bristol) until such time they have a more complete definition they accept and endorse the APPG one.'*

Bristol Council have included a 'terminology' section in their refreshed policy, 'including providing new definitions and disambiguation for lesser known terms such as "Afriphobia"'.

There is also reference to Black Lives Matter and the removal of Bristol's statue of Edward Colston, which the council says, 'have brought long-standing issues of race inequality even more sharply in to focus for the city'. They add:

> *'[S]ince this policy and strategy was originally published we have undertaken more work to acknowledge and address institutional racism, including independent support, facilitation and review which has helped inform our ongoing activities to improve practice across the council.'*

Calderdale Council – Labour

A January 2020 Calderdale Council cabinet report recommending adoption of both the IHRA and APPG definitions reads:

> *'The alternative option is not to adopt the IHRA and Islamophobia definitions. However, there is a risk associated with this; failure to adopt the definitions could have a significant impact on the council's reputation and relationship with communities in Calderdale.'*

This statement alone makes clear the council's reputational imperative, for fear of the 'significant impact', if they did not adopt the APPG's progressivist definition.

The report refers to nine Islamophobic incidents recorded between October 2018-September 2019. The minutes from the meeting dated 13 January 2020, confirming both definitions were adopted, reads:

> *'There had been an increase in hate rhetoric around Islamophobia and the more Councils who adopted the definitions, would send a clear message to the government that the more Councils were committed to tackling hate crime'.*

There is no attempt to quantify the 'increase' in 'hate rhetoric' mentioned, or consideration of a comparative historical timeframe. A councillor raised concerns about free speech, only to be informed there was 'no scope within the definitions to inhibit freedom of speech and/or criticism of a State.' Although it's not explicit, it appears the 'criticism of a State' is a veiled reference to Israel.

London Borough of Camden – Labour

In April 2019, Camden Council published a lengthy amended motion. The motion refers to hate crime figures from Tell MAMA which report a '593% increase in anti-Muslim hate in the week following the Christchurch outrage.' It also notes local hate crime data between 2015/16 and 2016/17, a period for which there has been an 11.9 per cent increase in racist and religious hate crime – from 616 to 689 cases. The motion notes, 'Muslim women are disproportionately targeted', but does not provide any more detail on the number of incidents or provide any specific local examples. The motion uses 'Islamophobia' and 'anti-Muslim' interchangeably, noting 'a large number of differing definitions of Islamophobia', which includes the APPG one. The motion brings attention to the fact that:

> *'...no definition has received international endorsement and the APPG's definition adopts a very different approach to others and to the IHRA definition of anti-Semitism adopted internationally and by this Council.'*

There are a series of points that the motion commits the council to implement, some rely on theories and contestable ideas. A selection is reproduced below:

- *'Call on the government to work with other governments and domestic partners to contribute to an internationally-recognised definition of Islamophobia, so that authorities and individuals can more effectively combat international hatred of Muslims.*
- *'Adopt such a definition as and when a definition has received widespread endorsement by European governments.*
- *'Work to combat anti-Muslim discrimination in the workplace, in education, in community organisations, and in its own authority to address the effects of any institutional and systematised hatred of Muslims, and to that end resolves to collect greater information on participation in activities to help root out what the Runnymede Trust calls the 'Muslim penalty' against employment, education, and social participation.*
- *'Work with schools and the Department for Education to ensure Muslim and other racial and religious minorities are sufficiently represented in the teaching of British history, including outside the history of colonialism, so that racial and religious minorities are appreciated by all as an integral part of our country's story and success.*
- *'Work with the police and community leaders to reassure all Muslims in the borough in preparation for Ramadan in May 2019.*
- *'Lobby the government for resources to improve security for Mosques in Camden.'*

Source: London Borough of Camden Council Meeting minutes 8 April 2019 – obtained via FoI.

Croydon council – No Overall Control

Notably the minutes from a meeting on 13 December 2021, pointed out how one councillor:

> *'[S]tated that the existing anti-racism measures in law were not equipped to deal with Islamophobia and that defining Islamophobia was a first step towards addressing it. The APPG on British Muslim definition had been backed by hundreds of organisations including the Muslim Council of Britain, yet there were still no changes in law.'*

This statement is remarkable, as it is already against the law to discriminate against anyone because of their religion or belief, and the Equality Act 2010 is clear that no one should be discriminated against because of their race too. Moreover, race discrimination includes the following:

- Colour;
- Nationality;
- Ethnic origin; and
- National origin.

All faiths and none have equal protection under law. The councillor may not have been informed that the APPG Islamophobia definition adopted by the council (like the IHRA antisemitism definition) is not legally binding, so cannot challenge the primacy of statute in any case.[130]

The minutes also include the 'lived experience' of a council member, with a broad subjective statement about a section of the Croydon community.

The minutes reveal how another councillor also spoke of his personal experience and that of the Muslim community, highlighting:

> *'...the fear that was experienced in just going about in the community. There was also feeling amongst younger member of the Muslim community that there would never be acceptance of them in wider society. He continued by stating that he was proud that the borough had tabled the motion and supported it.'*

Although the councillor's 'lived experience' paints a difficult picture and one which deserves sympathy, the reality is no one individual speaks for the experience of the entire community.

Another councillor brought attention to:

> *'[T]he online Islamophobia abuse with a huge number of people using fake identities and the widespread availability of white supremacist culture and the spread of fake news accusing the Muslim community of spreading Covid.'*

Whilst there is of course online targeting of minority communities, this would be attributable to social media users operating across the globe. It would be helpful to understand what constitutes 'online Islamophobia', as this isn't clear from the minutes. The broader narrative paints a simplistic and binary view of society – primarily 'white supremacists' targeting minorities, in this case, Muslims. In reality, social cohesion and community tensions are far more complex and convoluted – take the Hindu and Muslim civil unrest in Leicester last year, Sikh-Muslim violence in Slough, London and the Midlands in the nineties, sectarianism within the British Muslim community itself, or the 'hate crime' committed by a Muslim man against a Sikh temple (gurdwara) in Derby in 2020 as examples.[131]

130 *Hansard*, HC Deb. vol. 700, 9 September 2021. Available at: hansard.parliament.uk/commons/2021-09-09/debates/B2667B41-FDA9-4BFD-BCD3-AFD4AF5165FD/DefinitionOfIslamophobia#:~:text=Additionally%2C%20it%20has%20been%20repeatedly,and%20therefore%20it%20does%20not (Accessed: 26 July 2023).

131 Naylor, M. (2020) 'Derby 'Sikh temple knifeman' may face attempted murder charge', *Derbyshire Live*, 24 June. Available at: derbytelegraph.co.uk/news/derby-news/derby-sikh-temple-knifeman-face-4259193 (Accessed: 26 July 2023).

London Borough of Ealing – Labour

Ealing Council adopted both the IHRA and APPG in the same meeting in June 2019. Notably, an external petitioner lobbied to prevent adoption of the IHRA definition. The minutes note the contents of the petition:

> *'... on behalf of the West London Revolutionary Communist Group, presented a petition signed by 572 signatories stating 'Solidarity with Palestine! No to IHRA! We the undersigned declare the following: We are opposed to any move by Ealing London Borough Council to adopt the IHRA definition of anti-Semitism. Such a motion should be voted down by all councillors. Anti-Zionism is not anti-Semitism. The adoption of the IHRA definition by any public body or political party harms solidarity with Palestine.'*

Despite the petitioning, a council motion to adopt both definitions under the title, 'Standing Against Racism and Discrimination in Ealing', states:

> *'This Council adopts the definition of antisemitism, including its examples, as set out by the International Holocaust Remembrance Alliance, and adopts the definition of Islamophobia, including its examples, as set out by the All-Party Parliamentary Group on British Muslims. This Council condemns all forms of racism, Islamophobia, antisemitism, homophobia, transphobia, ageism, pregnancy and maternity discrimination, ableism and sexism and reaffirms our commitment to fighting against them.'*

London Borough of Hackney – Labour

- *'Personal reference was made to her [the councillor's] experience of Islamophobia as a young woman with unacceptable comments, discrimination at work, citing the example of people not sitting next to Muslims on public transport, or moving away if they began to read the Koran. These had become every day experiences for Muslims.*
- *'[The Councillor's] religion had taught her to love, respect and care for everyone. Yet, Muslims continued to be considered to be an attack on the British way of life.*
- *'There was a rise in islamophobia, extremism and right wing terrorism with negative comments made by politicians. In relation to the media, a recent study found that 59% of headlines showed Muslims in a negative light, using words such as terrorism. She considered that the increase in hatred, misconception and scaremongering by the media, right-wing extremists and even politicians was damaging to the way of life of this country.*
- *'Disappointment was expressed that Islam had been misconstrued and used by racists to create fear and promote their agenda for the future. She said that right wing terrorism was everywhere. A study in 2019 showed that the far right was tapping into political rage.*
- *'[The Councillor] passionately relayed what it felt like having to think twice whilst using public transport, particularly at peak/busy periods and expressed concerns about her personal safety because of her religion and choice to wear the hijab. She told Council that she should not have to have such thoughts cross her mind.'*

Source: London Borough of Hackney meeting minutes, 22 January 2020 – obtained via FoI.

It is of course sad to hear about individual fears about personal safety when using public transport. Women more broadly, travellers with disabilities and the elderly are also likely to have similar concerns when travelling too. The claim that, 'right wing terrorism was everywhere' doesn't appear to be quantified nor substantiated in the minutes. There is no mention of Islamic extremism in the minutes. Although the councillor's interpretation of her faith is to be respected, there are alternative interpretations, ones for example which result in the persecution and subjugation of women and minority faiths in countries like Afghanistan, Pakistan, and Iran, and by the transnational terror group known as The Islamic State of Iraq and the Levant, or ISIS.

London Borough of Haringey – Labour

The minutes from a meeting dated 20 May 2019 include councillors' reference to:

> *'[R]eal-life experiences and personal accounts of Islamophobia. They [two councillors] spoke of the likely underreporting of hate crimes connected with islamophobia and how this situation was getting much worse for the Muslim community'.*

The minutes note the New Zealand and Finsbury Park terrorist attacks, which 'highlighted the severe Islamophobic attacks that Muslim communities around the world are faced with'.

The council minutes record the following statements on adoption of the APPG definition:

'Council believes:

'1. That Muslims are valued members of the community in Haringey and of the United Kingdom.

'2. That Islamophobia has no place in Haringey, or in our wider society.

'3. That fears that applying the APPG definition will constrain freedom of speech are misplaced. Islamophobia Defined explicitly defends the right of Muslims and non-Muslims to engage in the "criticism, debate and free discussion of Islam as a religion", whilst setting out criteria to distinguish that from "the victimisation of Muslims through the targeting of expressions of Muslimness to deny or impair their fundamental freedoms and human rights".

'Council resolves:

'1. To welcome, endorse and adopt the All-Party Parliamentary Group on British Muslims' definition of Islamophobia.

'2. To contact the Members of Parliament for Tottenham and Hornsey & Wood Green and ask them to lobby the Government to adopt the All-Party Parliamentary Group on British Muslims' definition of Islamophobia.

'3. To condemn all bigotry and any discrimination on the basis of ethnicity, religion, denomination or any characteristic protected by the Equality Act.'

Source: London Borough of Haringey council meeting minutes, 20 May 2019 – obtained via FoI.

As previously discussed, the statement that the APPG definition will not constrain free speech is highly contested. But surprisingly, no counter argument is recorded in the council minutes, unlike the robust and balanced briefing provided to councillors in Aberdeenshire. Moreover, as Stephen Evans points out, the NSS's central concern with the definition is the word 'Islamophobia' itself, which 'conflates criticism of Islam or Islamic practices with hatred of Muslims.' Moreover, the term 'Muslimness' is also contested, as observed by Sara Khan, Baroness Falkner and, significantly, Muslims in Bradford who came up with an alternative definition.

Wales

Twenty-one FoIs were filed for local authorities in Wales. There is data for all local authorities, bar Newport. A total of six councils in Wales have adopted the IHRA definition – that constitutes 27.3 per cent of Welsh councils:

- Bridgend County Borough Council;
- Caerphilly County Borough Council;
- Cardiff Council;

- Carmarthenshire County Council;
- Flintshire County Council; and
- Rhondda Cynon Taf County Borough Council.

The documents obtained through FoI reveal that:

> *'In July 2021 all Leaders of Labour run councils were sent a letter from the Chair of the Labour Party urging them to demonstrate their commitment to supporting the Muslim community and working with them to root out Islamophobia wherever it rears its head by adopting the All Party Parliamentary Group (APPG) on British Muslims' definition of Islamophobia.'*

Five Welsh councils have adopted the APPG definition, which equates to 22.7 per cent of local authorities:

- Bridgend County Borough Council;
- Cardiff Council;
- Flintshire County Council;
- Rhondda Cynon Taf County Borough Council; and
- City and County of Swansea.

Cardiff has the highest proportion of Muslims, at 9.3 per cent – with Swansea recording the second highest, at 3.2 per cent, and Bridgend and Flintshire joint lowest, at 0.5 per cent, according to the latest 2021 census data. So, both areas with higher and lower Muslim populations have adopted the definition. Notably, Swansea adopted the APPG definition, but not the government endorsed IHRA, which is currently being considered by the board.

Bridgend – Labour

A Bridgend County Borough Council report to the Cabinet Committee Equalities (report of the Chief Executive) dated 8 November 2021 on considering the APPG definition reads:

> *'Without a working definition, Islamophobia is often misunderstood, ignored and even allowed to take place openly across society. To understand any kind of prejudice or hatred, one has to understand how it manifests. One example of this can be seen with the story of the nursery school places and the SNP Minister Humza Yousaf. - Humza Yousaf reports nursery over discrimination fears – BBC News.'*

This is a peculiar case to cite in an official document, given that the claim had not concluded or come to any form of settlement at the time. In February 2023, it was reported that Mr Yousaf and his wife dropped the discrimination case against the nursery. A news report said the nursery:

> *'... have always denied wrongdoing and vowed to fight back against the couple if the case went to court. However, it has been revealed that the case has been dropped. The owner of the nursery has revealed that she feels "vindicated" by the result as they were always adamant that they had been falsely accused.'*[132]

It appears the Bridgend Council briefing had prematurely concluded that Mr Yousaf's family had faced prejudice, citing it as an example to 'understand how it (Islamophobia) manifests.' On the Yousaf family nursery case, the briefing document concludes:

> *'Often this kind of day to day Islamophobia is ignored because Islamophobia is only seen as hatred such as verbal or physical attacks on individuals.'*

132 Walker, D. (2023) 'Embarrassment for Humza Yousaf and his wife as they drop high-profile legal action against nursery', *Scottish Daily Express*, 7 February. Available at: scottishdailyexpress.co.uk/news/politics/embarrassment-humza-yousaf-wife-drop-29157193 (Accessed: 26 July 2023).

Citing unsubstantiated claims of Islamophobia without evidence does not put the council's briefing document in a positive light.

The report also refers to 'both conscious and unconscious biases' towards the Muslim community, which stems directly from contested CRT. The belief that implicit, unconscious prejudice is a driver of modern racial inequality is central to the controversial academic discipline of CRT. This has clearly been extended to Islamophobia, as a 'type of racism'. However, remarkably, the document does not consider any reasons not to adopt the definition, and seems to be heavily one sided, that is, there is no mention of balancing free speech, or the challenge that accusations of 'Islamophobia' bring to counterextremism efforts by inhibiting referrals to Prevent, nor mention of the fact that the government rejected the said definition. The document stresses rather that, 'The adoption of the APPG definition of Islamophobia will signal to Muslim communities that there is a willingness to tackle Islamophobia.' Notably the document excises the same working example as Harlow and Salford, and limits this to 'Using the symbols and images associated with classic Islamophobia' only. Again, it is not clear why this decision has been made.

Swansea – Labour

The Council document titled 'Notion of Motion – Adopting a Definition of Islamophobia', dated 3 November 2022, indicates as in Harlow, Salford, and Bridgend – the same working example, 'Using the symbols and images associated with classic Islamophobia', which has been edited down from the original version published in *Islamophobia Defined*.

Cardiff – Labour

The Notice of Motion proposed by the councillor includes the APPG definition. Minutes from the meeting on 24 November 2022 include the following:

> *'Motion*
>
> *'This Council believes that:*
>
> - *'Adopting a definition of Islamophobia is essential to tackling Islamophobia in a targeted and effective manner.*
> - *'Without a definition of Islamophobia, one cannot identify how Islamophobia manifests itself and functions and therefore, cannot devise meaningful strategies to address it.*
>
> *'This Council resolves to:*
>
> - *'Adopt the APPG definition of Islamophobia, accompanied by the Coalition Against Islamophobia's explanatory guidelines to provide a more holistic understanding of Islamophobia.*
> - *'Work with Cardiff schools, public transport companies, the South Wales police force, and other public and private bodies to tackle Islamophobia at a local level, in support of the wider work responding to the Race Equality Task Force recommendations.*
> - *'Take further steps to tackle and raise awareness of Islamophobia, such as training and events on how to tackle Islamophobia, during Islamophobia Awareness Month (November)*
> - *'Collaborate with the local Muslim community to challenge Islamophobia and to meet their needs such that they are encouraged to participate in public life and all aspects of life such as education, employment, training and public services.*
> - *'Ensure Cardiff Council's workforce is diverse and inclusive through engaging with training programmes to tackle Islamophobia and unconscious bias.*
> - *'Work with other local stakeholders such as the local MPs to raise awareness of Islamophobia in parliament and urge the UK Government to adopt the APPG definition of Islamophobia'*
>
> Source: Cardiff Council meeting minutes, 24 November 2022 – obtained via FoI.

Flintshire – No Overall Control

The cabinet meeting minutes from a 21 September 2021 meeting confirm that both the IHRA and APPG definitions were adopted at the same time.

Scotland

There is a total of 32 councils in Scotland. Thirty FoI requests were put in and all of them replied. Eleven councils confirmed that they had adopted the IHRA definition, which constitutes 34.4 per cent of local authorities:

- Aberdeen City Council;
- Dumfries and Galloway Council;
- Dundee City Council;
- East Renfrewshire Council;
- Edinburgh City Council;
- Glasgow City Council;
- Moray Council;
- Perth and Kinross Council;
- Renfrewshire Council;
- South Lanarkshire Council; and
- West Lothian Council.

Eight local authorities in Scotland confirmed that they adopted the APPG definition, which equates to 25 per cent of local authorities:

- Dundee City Council;
- East Ayrshire Council;
- Glasgow City Council;
- Inverclyde Council;
- Moray Council;
- Perth and Kinross Council;
- South Lanarkshire Council; and
- West Lothian Council.

Dundee City Council – SNP

One of the most interesting findings from Dundee City Council's FoI disclosure is that the current First Minister Yousaf's wife, Councillor El-Nakla, led the adoption of the APPG definition in Dundee City Council.

The minutes of the meeting on 21 November 2022 record the following:

> *'This Item was placed on the agenda at the request of Councillor El-Nakla who asked the Committee to adopt the All-Party Parliamentary Group on British Muslims definition of Islamophobia.*
>
> *'Thereafter, the Committee resolved the following: -*
>
> *'Islamophobia is rooted in racism and is a type of racism that targets expressions of Muslimness or perceived Muslimness - together with the explanatory guidelines put forward by the Coalition Against Islamophobia.*
>
> *'Faith organisations have a commitment to serve their communities, and there are many examples in Dundee of faith organisations taking social action, running local initiatives and providing services which make a positive impact on some of the most vulnerable people in our society.*
>
> *'Dundee has a very positive record of working within our communities and educational services to tackle religious intolerance. We must continue to raise awareness and work with stakeholders to ensure that Dundee's diverse communities are supported.*

'Islamophobia is a growing issue, both locally and nationally, as a public inquiry by the Scottish Parliaments Cross-Party Group (CPG) on Tackling Islamophobia found that approximately 80% of Muslims in Scotland have experienced Islamophobia directly.

'Council recognises the importance of faith groups across Dundee and recognises the vital role that they play within our communities and for the benefit of our communities.

'Council reiterates our commitment through the Faith Covenant (Report: 59-2020), adopted at Policy and Resources Committee on 24th February 2020 to: -

- *'Work with faith communities, through a joint working group of officers and faith representatives and report back on key recommendations.*
- *'Continue to build relationships and trust with faith groups.*
- *'Adopt strategies for the engagement and support of faith communities.*
- *'Share training and learning opportunities.*
- *'Work to tackle religious intolerance, in all of its forms.*

'Council further agrees that: -

- *'Adopting a definition of Islamophobia is essential to tackling Islamophobia in a targeted and effective manner.*
- *'Without a definition of Islamophobia, one cannot identify how Islamophobia manifests itself and functions and therefore, cannot devise meaningful strategies to address it.*
- *'The APPG definition should be accompanied by the Coalition Against Islamophobias explanatory guidelines to provide a more holistic understanding of Islamophobia.'*

Source: Dundee City Council's Policy & Resources Committee meeting minutes, 21 November 2022 – obtained via FoI.

Glasgow – No Overall Control

Minutes of the motion dated 27 October 2022 show it was put forward by two councillors, with an amendment put forward by two others. The final, agreed motion is reproduced below:

'Glasgow has a strong recent history of, and flourishing reputation for, promoting cohesion and welcoming people from all over the world. Council reaffirms our determination to oppose racism and discrimination in all the forms in which they manifest themselves in Glasgow's daily life, institutions and wider society. Glasgow is proud of its growing diversity and this Council views this as an asset and source of great strength. Council recognises that Glasgow has been home to a significant Muslim population for generations and that our Muslim citizens are an integral part of all aspects of city life.

'Council notes the vile racist and Islamophobic abuse recently targeted at pupils of St. Albert's Primary School in the City and condemns that abuse unreservedly. Council reiterates its belief that racism has no place in our City, and expresses its wholehearted support to the affected pupils, teachers, staff and wider community affected by these comments. Council further notes the publication of the 'Report of the inquiry into Islamophobia in Scotland' by the Tackling Islamophobia CPG which found that of Muslim respondents 82% with a Glasgow postcode identified that Islamophobia is getting worse. Respondents said that these incidents happened at work, at school, at college or university. Taken together, this demonstrates that Glasgow still has much to do to tackle the scourge of racism. Council unequivocally condemns prejudice and intolerance in all forms. Council therefore welcomes, endorses and adopts the working APPG (All-Party Parliamentary Group) definition of Islamophobia, including all of its examples in full, cited as follows. (all the Islamophobia Defined report's working examples are subsequently included in full)

'Council agrees to continue to tackle hate crime and Islamophobia in partnership with communities, Police Scotland and other stakeholders. Council further agrees as a first step to support Islamophobia Awareness Month in November 2022 to bring understanding and attention to the scourge of Islamophobia and encourage better reporting of incidents to the police. Council also instructs that a paper be brought to Safe Glasgow detailing how the APPG definition can be embedded in its work and consider how Safe Glasgow can raise awareness of crime motivated by prejudice on the grounds of actual or perceived religion.'

Source: Glasgow City Council meeting minutes, 27 October 2022 – obtained via FoI.

Inverclyde – No Overall Control

A report to the Council by the Head of Legal & Democratic Services, dated 30 June 2022 under the subject: 'Definition of Islamophobia – Request by Councillor McCabe on behalf of Muslim Engagement and Development', provides some fascinating insights into the lobbying of Scottish councils. An appendix provides a copy of an open letter (dated 23 February 2022) 'urging' adoption of the APPG by Scottish councils, which has a significant number of signatories – the first being the advocacy group MEND. The appendix also provides details of The Campaign Against Islamophobia guidelines on Islamophobia, with a hyperlink to a website. The document expresses some reservation only insofar as it notes:

> *'For some, the definition may not be clear and Muslimness may be a concept that many people are not familiar with. In addition, it should be noted that there are other definitions of Islamophobia.'*

It however makes a single recommendation: 'That the Council considers the request by Councillor McCabe on behalf of Muslim Engagement and Development'.

Moray Council – No Overall Control

A section from the minutes from the 1 February 2022 are reproduced below:

'Definition of Islamophobia

'Councillor Leadbitter, seconded by Councillor Morrison, proposed a Motion in the following terms:

'Council notes the request made to the Council Leader by Muslim Engagement & Development (MEND), backed by 32 community, charitable and religious organisations, that Moray Council adopt the All Party Parliamentary Group (APPG) on British Muslims definition of Islamophobia, which has also been accepted by all political parties in the Scottish Parliament.

'Council considers that adopting the APPG definition of islamophobia will assist Moray Council in meeting all three elements of its public sector equality duties on the grounds of race and religion. It demonstrates a proactive consideration by the council of the need to:

- *'Eliminate discrimination, harassment, victimisation and other conduct prohibited by the Equality Act 2010 on the grounds of race and religion in relation to the Muslim Population*
- *'Promote equality of opportunity on those grounds*
- *'Fosters good relations between the Muslim population and other groups in our Community Council therefore agrees to adopt the APPG definition of Islamophobia, which states:*

'"Islamophobia is rooted in racism and is a type of racism that targets expressions of Muslimness or perceived Muslimness."'

Source: Moray Council meeting minutes, 15 March 2022 – obtained via FoI.

Although the council's interpretation of meeting their Public Sector Equality duties by adopting the APPG definition are of course highly debatable, one interesting point that came out of the discussion was some members talked of having experienced 'Anglophobia' whilst living in Scotland. The minutes record that this 'was considered to be unacceptable and it was queried whether the Council's intolerance to Anglophobia could be included in the motion.'

Councillor Leadbitter said any discrimination against race or religion was unacceptable, but he did not feel Anglophobia should be included in a motion on Islamophobia. He said he was not averse to consider an Anglophobia definition within Council policy, 'using the correct definition', which was not available at the time.

These minutes highlight the clear problem with exclusive hate crime definitions for specific groups at the expense of others. Rather than 'fostering good relations', this example within the council itself demonstrates how it can be divisive and drives a negative culture of competitive grievance. After all, it is quite reasonable to question why one group has a special endorsed definition, and another does not – do they not count? Rather than promote 'good relations', there is a danger that councils are inadvertently nurturing a culture of grievance and rivalry between identity groups.

West Lothian Council – No Overall Control

A report on the APPG definition by Corporate Services dated 7 September 2021 refers to the development of the working definition and cites the involvement of the Network of Sikh Organisations and The National Secular Society (both gave evidence to the APPG). However, it oddly does not refer to opposition to the APPG definition by the named groups as contributors to the Civitas anthology (2019) or accompanying letter to the Home Secretary.

It refers to the setting up in April 2018 of the Scottish Parliament's Cross-Party Group (CPG) on tackling Islamophobia, and an inquiry into Islamophobia in Scotland which supported the APPG definition, and one of the recommendations being that the Scottish government adopt a formal definition of Islamophobia.

The report notes:

> *'[I]f the definition is adopted it will require a commitment to ensuring a shared understanding of its meaning within the council and wider community. For some the above definition may not be clear. Muslimness may be a concept that many people are not familiar with.'*

It acknowledges multiple definitions of Islamophobia, including the Runnymede Trust one.

Conclusions

There has clearly been a considerable amount of lobbying going on to influence the adoption of the APPG Islamophobia definition by local government. Despite government rejection, the levels of adoption are small but significant. Where the issue of free speech has been raised by some councillors, it has largely been dismissed, except for some examples where the NSS has intervened. Questions about the meaning of 'Muslimness' have been raised several times, and its vagueness continues to be problematic as it conflates practices which all people may not agree with on legitimate grounds.

The research brings into question whether local councils did the necessary due diligence and scrutiny, before making decisions to adopt. With a few notable exceptions, broadly, it appears not. Aberdeenshire certainly did; other briefing documents appear to be one-sided, and sparse on outlining reasons why not to adopt. This is troubling and shows an element of bias. As we have seen, one council absurdly cites the reputational impact of not adopting as grounds to adopt. What's more troubling is akin to allegations of 'institutional racism'; once terms like Islamophobia are controlled, power is created over institutions, and then ultimately over individuals. In the end, this leads to a culture of self-censorship, and a 'tide of little erosions' of free speech on matters of fundamental importance, not least an honest conversation about public policies relating to faith or religion, or basic historical truths.

It is therefore recommended that the following actions be taken.

Recommendations

- Councils affirm the principle of free speech as a motion in light of the APPG definition adoption, to includes reference to section 29J of the Public Order Act 1986, which under 'Protection of freedom of expression' reads:

  'Nothing in this Part shall be read or given effect in a way which prohibits or restricts discussion, criticism or expressions of antipathy, dislike, ridicule, insult or abuse of particular religions or the beliefs or practices of their adherents, or of any other belief system or the beliefs or practices of its adherents, or proselytising or urging adherents of a different religion or belief system to cease practising their religion or belief system.'[133]

- Councils must promote inclusivity with a broader equality consideration so that one body of law applies to all, and these should be reflected to mirror existing provisions for Muslims and Jews in internal policies, delivery of services, and regularly kept under review. Embedding such considerations on a level pegging into equalities policy should be a bare minimum requirement.
- Councils who've adopted the APPG Islamophobia definition must give their employees reassurance that they can talk freely about historical truths, and be able to criticise religion, without being accused of being 'racist'.
- Councils should affirm that the mere accusation of 'Islamophobia' can indeed have extremely dangerous consequences for accused individuals, like the troubling case of Professor Greer.
- There should be one single agreed definition of Islamophobia used across all local authorities in England, Wales, and Scotland. An 'anti-Muslim' hate crime definition would be preferable due to the ambiguity of the word 'Islamophobia'.

133 UK Government (1986) *Public Order Act 1986*. Available at: legislation.gov.uk/ukpga/1986/64/section/29J/1991-02-01 (Accessed: 26 July 2023).

- Councils must provide a clear statement that they will treat all faiths/beliefs and protected groups equally with 'due regard' under the Public Sector Equality Duties and are not to be seen to favour one group over another. This could involve updating policy to reflect examples of anti-Christian, anti-Hindu, anti-Sikh, and anti-Atheist hate crime, which also include cases where some victims are mistaken to be Muslim extremists.
- Councils should affirm the principle that no 'characteristics' should receive special legal protection or privilege, that violates the principle of equality under the law.
- Councils who have adopted the APPG definition must clearly define what they mean by 'Muslimness' and provide specific examples with case studies.
- Councils should scrap all divisive equality, diversity and inclusion training, and especially unconscious bias training.
- The Department for Levelling Up, Housing & Communities should make a statement on the levels of adoption of the APPG Islamophobia definition by local authorities in England and Wales despite the government's rejection.
- Police should share data on the 'perceived' versus 'actual' victim of hate crime for Islamophobic hate crimes recorded.
- The Government should reaffirm the principle of equality before the law for all.

About Civitas: The Institute for the Study of Civil Society

- We facilitate informed public debate by providing accurate factual information on the social issues of the day, publishing informed comment and analysis, and bringing together leading protagonists in open discussion. Civitas never takes a corporate view on any of the issues tackled during the course of this work. Our current focus is on issues such as education, health, crime, social security, manufacturing, the abuse of human rights law, and the European Union.
- We ensure that there is strong evidence for all our conclusions and present the evidence in a balanced and objective way. Our publications are usually refereed by independent commentators, who may be academics or experts in their field.
- We strive to benefit public debate through independent research, reasoned argument, lucid explanation and open discussion. We stand apart from party politics and transitory intellectual fashions.
- Uniquely among think tanks, we play an active, practical part in rebuilding civil society by running schools on Saturdays and after-school hours so that children who are falling behind at school can achieve their full potential.

Subscriptions and Membership (UK only)

If you would like to stay abreast of Civitas' latest work, you can have all of our books delivered to your door as soon as they are published. New subscribers receive a free copy of Roger Bootle's book, *The AI Economy: Work, Wealth and Welfare in the Robot Age* and Daniel Bentley's book, *The Land Question* on fixing the dysfunction at the root of the housing crisis. For those who would like to support our work further and get involved in our Westminster events, we have a variety of Subscription and Membership options available:

www.civitasonline.org.uk/product-category/subscriptions

We regret that we are unable to post items to non-UK residents, although all of our publications are individually available via our Civitas Book Store (www.civitasonline.org.uk) and in most cases on Amazon.

Renewals for Existing Members

If you are an existing member wishing to renew with ease and convenience, please do select one of the subscription or membership options that most closely meets your requirements.

Make a Donation

If you like our work and would like to help see it continue, please consider making a donation. A contribution of any amount, big or small, will help us advance our research and educational activities. You can make a donation by getting in touch (020 7799 6677) or sending a simple email to info@civitas.org.uk so that we can come back to you.

Supporters of Civitas

Because we want to reach as wide an audience as possible, our subscription and membership fees are set as low as possible and barely meet printing and postage expenses. To meet the costs of producing our research and conducting our educational projects, we rely entirely on the goodwill and generosity of people who value our work.

If you would like to support our work on a rolling basis, there is a variety of advanced membership levels on offer. Supporters of Civitas have the opportunity to become more deeply engaged with the work their philanthropy makes possible.

You can pay by selecting a membership or subscription option and we will be in contact. Alternatively, just call us on +44 (0)20 7799 6677 or email info@civitas.org.uk and we can discuss your options.